Praise for
Written on Water

"What a treat to spend time in Randy Spencer's guide canoe without leaving your chair. If I hadn't met a few of his Downeast characters, I'd swear he was making them up! Just plain wonderful reading!"

—**Peter Mehegan**, co-host of WCVB-TV's *Chronicle*

"These dispatches from a remote corner of Maine are a delight to read. Randy Spencer's characters—fishing guides, junk dealers, small-town sheriffs, pot growers, boat builders and trappers, to name just a few— are as pungent as spruce sap. But *Written on Water* is more than a gallery of memorable Mainers—it's a celebration of a passing way of life."

—**Lou Ureneck**, Author, Professor and Winner of National Outdoor Book Award and Yankee Quill Award

WRITTEN ON WATER

CHARACTERS AND MYSTERIES
FROM MAINE'S BACK OF BEYOND

RANDY SPENCER

RIVERCLIFF
BOOKS & MEDIA

Rivercliff Books & Media
an Imprint of Wetware Media, LLC

www.rivercliffbooks.com

Cover design by Chris & Con Designs

ISBN: 978-1-954566-01-9

Publisher's Cataloging-in-Publication data

Names: Spencer, Randy, author.
Title: Written on water : characters and mysteries
from Maine's back of beyond / Randy Spencer.
Description: Boulder, CO: Rivercliff Books & Media, 2021.
Identifiers: LCCN: 2021945824 | ISBN: 978-1-954566-
01-9 (paperback) | 978-1-954566-02-6 (ebook)
Subjects: LCSH Spencer, Randy. | Fishing guides--
Maine--Biography. | Fishing--Maine--Grand Lake
Stream (Me.). | Fishing--Maine--History. | BISAC
BIOGRAPHY & AUTOBIOGRAPHY / Personal
Memoirs | SPORTS & RECREATION / Fishing
Classification: LCC SH503 .S64 2021 | DDC 799.1/092--dc23

Dedicated to Edith Sprague, who has been a living library
and a rich resource of humor, rumor, and the truth
throughout the 40 years of our friendship.

Contents

Acknowledgments

My work with the Passamaquoddy Tribe as a digital archivist has helped me understand what an oral history is. If it were taught in the classroom to children, they would probably find it far more interesting than the standard history texts. This is because they could relate to it. Their oral history would be full of people like them, navigating similar struggles and challenges, though in another time, and it would be delivered to them in rhyme, in songs, sometimes even in dances. I am grateful for the opportunity to have listened to more than one hundred hours of interviews with tribal elders during the process of digitizing them and thereby to have gained some insight into the value of these spoken accounts.

Since timing is everything, I'm thankful that I arrived on the scene in this particular fishing town before the previous generation of guides was gone. I loved nothing more than listening to them, sometimes with a notepad and pen, or going with them on outdoor adventures and watching how they moved. Having lived their whole lives in the outdoors, they were attuned to it in ways difficult to describe. A wild animal walks through the woods, always knowing where it is. In the water, it knows how to pace itself, stay afloat and conserve energy. It was something like that with these old guides.

I'm grateful to those who are attempting, against steep odds, to carry on those traditions established by previous generations. They've got a mountain to climb, but they'll do it because it's who they are. If they're right for the job, they'll be sought out by complete strangers destined to become friends.

When a manuscript finds its proper home, it's a feeling on the part of the author, like no other. With Rivercliff, that connection was immediate. Publisher Lisa Duff, editor Carol Stanley, and copy editor Susannah Davies responded to this work with a deep understanding and a clear view of the way forward. My thanks to them for this rare experience.

Finally, to my first readers, Shelley Spencer and Lewis Bates "Toby" Codding IV, I say thank you once more. You are where my trust begins, and my gratitude continues.

Preface

The stories compiled here all take place against a backdrop of unparalleled natural resources in America's most forested state. Eighty-nine percent of Maine is woodland. Apart from its iconic coastline, it boasts over six thousand lakes and ponds, as well as countless rivers, streams, and flowages. That was what first drew outdoor "sports" here from all points of the compass in the days when rail ruled. And the good news is that the pristine wilderness they boarded trains and rode great distances to experience a century ago is still here, and it is largely unchanged.

Industrialists, inventors, sports celebrities, even presidents came to breathe the clean air and smell the balsam fir while angling for salmon and trout or stalking big game in the fall. It was an appealing destination where prominent people could trade in their high profile for a low one and enjoy nature nearly anonymously. Then, as now, sports who came from away to fish a dizzying assortment of choice waters, or to hunt huge, untamed tracts of game habitat, spent most of their time with a guide. Out of this, some celebrated relationships grew.

Joe Polis guided Henry David Thoreau through the treks and adventures that would become Thoreau's classic, *The Maine Woods*. Bill Sewall guided Rough Rider and president Teddy Roosevelt from the time he was nineteen until well into his presidency. Passamaquoddy guide Joe Mell traipsed these environs with famed photographer William Underwood, yielding some of the works now displayed at the Smithsonian. When fabled World War II Medal of Honor recipient Jimmy Doolittle died at age ninety-six, he'd fished most of the years since the war with Grand Lake Stream guide Val Moore. They corresponded faithfully during the off-season.

This interaction between local guides and interesting people from all walks of life produced a rich oral history, passed down in the form of stories, poems, and sometimes songs among guides and townsfolk. They are treasures that exist in the vault of memory. That tradition is still alive today, looking remarkably like it did when it began at the start of the twentieth century. Guides still show up in Grand Laker canoes loaded with picnic baskets, firewood, and tackle to create days that go into that vault, adding to the deep repository that is our collective archive.

Oral history is not where to look for facts or certainty. It's where to go for culture, color, and the legacies of often unsung storytellers, balladeers, and poets. Is all of what you will find the unadulterated truth? The recipients, the listeners to whom these stories are passed down, would answer, "That misses the point." We may say that all of it is based on true events, just as all of the stories in this volume are. But the real function of an oral history is to breathe life and a sense of belonging into succeeding generations. It is the common thread that runs through places like Grand Lake Stream, Maine, providing context in the present and a connection to the past.

I've given new names to some of the characters who are still alive in order to steer unwelcome scrutiny away from them. When the true names of the deceased are used, it is by way of tribute to them. Every account you will read is, unavoidably, approximate. Their purpose here is to demonstrate that such places and such people really do still exist. These stories change shape and form with the passage of time. They are, after all, written on water.

1

The Old Cowboy

I knew him as the Old Cowboy. By the time he was sixty-eight years old, he was in a wheelchair, wearing down the linoleum from the kitchen to the living room in his tiny, one-bedroom house in Grand Lake Stream. He didn't use the bedroom. He opted instead for the couch in the living room, where he could watch one of the three stations the rabbit ears on his Zenith TV set picked up. He could also keep the fire going in the Jøtul woodstove in the opposite corner of the room. His caregiver, Terry, filled the wood box in the kitchen once a day during her three hours of cleaning, tidying, cooking, and washing. Several times a day, Cowboy wheeled out to the wood box, loaded up his lap with beech, birch, ash, or oak, and wheeled it back out to the stove.

That's what you would've seen had you stopped by, as many people did, for a mid-day visit. The next year, the couch was swapped out for a hospital bed, but he still managed to get himself out of that and into the wheelchair every morning, then back into bed every night. He still toileted himself, changed clothes on his own, and kept that woodstove dancing. Every visitor was received cordially, sharing town news as well as gossip, often indistinguishable from each other. For example, one early winter, Cowboy's uncle Gabe stopped by to tell him that Pop Moore's Bronco had partially gone through the ice in The Narrows while he was on his way to the Bernard camp in Junior Bay. Pop's Grand Lake Canoes are collectors' items now. He is in the Pantheon of local artisans who made canoes to last a lifetime. He had been the caretaker for that sprawling camp for decades. It was his custom always to be the first to chance a trip through The Narrows, and if he made it, the rest of West Grand Lake was pronounced safe. His judgment was so trusted that, the very next day, trucks and cars could be seen all over the fifteen thousand-acre sea of ice.

In this way, Cowboy kept up with what was going on in the tiny nook they all called a town. He had the last four digits of everyone's phone number written on the inside cover of the almost weightless local phone book, because all numbers began with the 796 prefix. The truth was, he didn't need to look any longer; those numbers lived in his brain, each with a name beside it, and when he needed to call someone, or just wanted to hear their voice, he picked up the receiver and dialed the number by heart.

Aunt Wilhelmina, Gabe's sister, had a part-time job knitting socks and baking cookies for her nephew, Cowboy. Very often, folks live such long lives in Grand Lake Stream that they become caretakers of their senior citizen children or other family members. Thus, Cowboy had relatives twenty and thirty years his senior looking in on him.

Despite all the visitors he received, despite the three hours a day with Terry, there would still have been plenty of time for boredom. Had that been the case, Cowboy's story would have been a much sadder one after he came down with chronic obstructive pulmonary disease, a debilitating lung condition. He appreciated breathing more than the average person because, all too often, he couldn't do it very well. He was determined to make the most of every breath from then on. He was the busiest non-working individual I've ever known, before or since.

Sometime after he was given his "sentence," as he liked to call his diagnosis, he embarked upon two brand-new careers: creator and curator. Cowboy had long flirted with the idea of hooking rugs with fine wool and making up his own designs. But as long as he was guiding and building homes and camps around the region, he never really got around to it. Once housebound and grounded in a wheelchair, he deemed his circumstances perfect for revisiting this dream. Terry brought him books and periodicals from the Calais Free Library. He researched where the best wools came from, as well as the best hooking tools: double curve scissors, fabric cutters, darning needles, and magnifying lamps.

Within a month, there were wools from Finland, Scotland, and Cape Breton, Nova Scotia, exploding in a burst of color all over the formerly dingy living room. A stretcher and shiny new tools sat on the low table in front of Cowboy's wheelchair. He had used his VA and disability benefits to get the materials he needed to launch his new career, saying, "The house is all paid for and the roof don't leak. What else am I gonna spend it on?"

After working out several different designs on a sketch pad with a lead pencil, Cowboy pitched into his first hooked rug. It was small, measuring about eighteen by twenty-four inches. Against a white backing, the words "Halfday Brookies" were boldly embossed in striking red wool. Some, I knew, might think it an odd choice of words for a hooked rug most likely meant to be hung like a tapestry. He knew what it meant, and I knew what it meant, but the average connoisseur of the woolen arts probably wouldn't. In spring and early summer, guided fishing days sometimes get rained out in the morning. The guide rarely makes this decision; he or she will fish in almost any conditions. Sometimes, when the rain is so heavy that it splashes six inches off the surface of the lake, certain sports give the signal to abort. On such days, some guides might suggest bushwhacking for brook trout. The forest canopy can relieve some of the rain's intensity, but the activity requires a certain level of physical stamina, because there's liable to be a hefty amount of hiking involved. The reward for all this effort can be well worth it. Wild, speckled trout inhabit almost any truly remote stream in this part of Maine. They are largely unfished, simply because they're so hard to get to. (Formerly bountiful trout streams beside newly paved roads are never long in earning the title, "formerly.")

Cowboy had shown me some of these out-of-the-way brooks and told me about others. "When the blackflies are at their worst," he always said, "that's the time to go." Even with hip boots on and half a bottle of Deet smeared over any exposed skin, I usually came back soaked and muddy with my eyes swollen shut. And yet, it was all worth it if you had five plump brook trout to show for it. It was just the ticket to round out the day for the eager, motivated sport who'd decided against bathing in a boat for eight hours. Thus the term "Halfday Brookies."

Cowboy continued this theme in tapestries that would be right at home in any camp, each one looking more polished and professional than the last. The next piece featured another fishing motif that would be known to any serious lake trout angler on West Grand Lake. The gray and brown letters spelling out "Togue Alley" look as if they're in relief against the lighter gray background. It refers to one of the deepest places in the lake, known to produce, year after year, some of the biggest togue (the Abenaki word for lake trout). The colors of wool Cowboy selected are the exact colors of this deep-water fish.

Cowboy's legs might have turned rickety and his lungs insubstantial, but his eyes were still good—his eyes and his mind. Apparently, there were still enough hours in a day to take up another interest of his in a big way, and that was country music. When famed documentarian Ken Burns made the film *Country Music*, he would've done well to consult Cowboy when he was still alive, or Cowboy's library after he was gone. The first thing he did was buy a stack of leather-bound cases, each of which held fifty cassette tapes, still very much in vogue in the 1980s. For each case, he bought a corresponding notebook. Cowboy's forte and great love was classic country music, not the cookie-cutter kind that was being churned out of Nashville by the latest pretty face under a big Stetson. "All hat and no cattle" was a favorite expression of his when he'd seen one of this ilk on his TV set.

Cowboy was more interested in "the real thing," as he put it: the ones the pretty faces wanted to emulate. The Sons of the Pioneers. The Louvin Brothers. Gene Autry. Tex Ritter. The Singing Brakeman, Jimmie Rodgers. Hank Williams Sr. Lefty Frizzell. The Singing Sheriff, Ferlin Husky. Patsy Cline. Hank Snow. Johnny Cash. And of course, the Baron of Country Music, Maine's own Dick Curless, and many, many more. Instead of setting up a recording studio in his living room, which was already full of rug hooking paraphernalia, Cowboy set a simple cassette recorder in front of his radio and hit "Record" every time something that he deemed worthy came on. There was a station out of Machias, Maine, that he listened to religiously, very often into the wee hours of the morning. "Old folks don't sleep much anyway," he'd tell me.

In twelve to eighteen hours a day of listening and recording, you can amass a lot of material. But this wasn't going to be a helter-skelter array of tunes with no rhyme or reason. Cowboy decided to be a chronicler and a curator. Artists belong to their own era, even if their music belongs to every era. He classified them according to their active years and also with respect to which "wing" of the art form they occupied, or in some cases, initiated. Bob Wills and his Texas Playboys, for example, were most often associated with Western swing, and so other artists or groups that fit within that framework went onto that cassette tape category with them. Spade Cooley, Asleep at the Wheel, Hank Thompson, and Commander Cody and His Lost Planet Airmen were all there in a leather-bound case, preserved for posterity.

In another was the Bakersfield sound, with Wynn Stewart, Buck Owens, Merle Haggard, and Dwight Yoakam. Then came the outlaw country movement, and Cowboy threw himself into the music of Waylon Jennings, Willie Nelson, Mickey Newbury, Jerry Jeff Walker, Bobby Bare, and others. Sum up the discography of these artists, and you begin to see how extensive this library was going to be. Each time I visited it had grown, and more cases had been added. Once, when I asked him what he thought he might do with this collection, he looked at me with an odd expression. "Do?" he said. "I'm doing it, right now." It was the listening, the assigning, the chronicling, and the amassing itself that not only kept him interested, but allowed his interest and appreciation to grow. I've known only one or two people in my life who could keep up with Cowboy in a conversation about country music. He was an opportunity missed by Ken Burns.

Sometimes it occurred to me when I watched Cowboy work that there was more to it than merely what met the eye. I'd known him for twenty years, and he'd shared a lot about his early life. Like the U.S. Army Air Corps' refusal to let him fly because of a heart arrhythmia after he'd passed aviation cadet school with flying colors. He would have been sent to either the European or the Pacific theater in World War II to fly bombing missions had they not picked up the anomaly in a routine physical. That snub stayed with him for the rest of his life, and we were never very far away from talking about it.

I knew that later, there were losses, estrangements, problems with drink, and things we tended not to belabor in our friendship. As the Willie Nelson line goes, "there's nothing I can do about it now," except maybe be as kind and generous a person as he could be with his limited resources and mobility. He gave away his masterworks with glee. All he wanted to know was that they'd be hung somewhere and be seen. He produced a mountain of hooked rugs and tapestries in the several years he had before his breathing became too restricted even for that activity.

It also gave him great joy to loan out his country music collection. It always came back intact. The DJs at the Machias radio station began to mention him on the air as one of the most knowledgeable fans of the station and of country music. This delighted him to no end.

Rarely did I come away from a visit with Cowboy during which I had not doubled over at least once at some story he'd told me. One time, when he was just out of high school, he'd come into a little bit of money when a relative died. He decided to treat himself and his best friend, Bill, to a trip to the big city. They caught a Greyhound bus out of Calais, Maine, one morning, and that night checked into the Copley Square Hotel in Boston. First thing the next morning, they went to a haberdasher and purchased new outfits, all on Cowboy's inheritance. The boys left a money trail everywhere they went: lunches at Durgin-Park where they fell in love with the Indian pudding, dinners at Fanueil Hall, shows in the theater district, and even a few jaunts through Boston's unwholesome Combat Zone to see things no kid growing up in the Maine woods could ever be prepared for.

While they walked through the gauntlet of professional women in the Combat Zone, Bill, suspicious by nature, but also mischievous, convinced Cowboy to strike up a deal with one of them. The prettiest one they could find also turned out to be the most accommodating. She readily agreed to meet Cowboy back at his room in Copley Square after being paid in full, up front. He was six inches off the ground and at a dead run all the way back to the hotel. Bill, who suspected what was going to happen, had to hide his glee. When one hour passed, then two, then three, it finally began to dawn on Cowboy that he'd been had, and Bill's hysterics were released. They'd always played pranks on each other, and this was Bill's best.

The money was gone after the three-day weekend, and it was a good thing they'd bought round-trip tickets. They barely had enough change for Cokes before they boarded their Greyhound at South Station. In line ahead of Bill as they were about to step up onto the bus was "a woman of considerable beam," as Cowboy put it. With her gigantic handbag added to her width, she took up the entire bus entrance. Cowboy, still smarting from Bill's prank, saw his moment. When the matronly lady got onto the second step and Bill onto the first, Cowboy reached around Bill, who was looking up, and goosed the poor, unsuspecting woman. She let out a shriek that scared the bus driver out of his seat, wheeled around to her left, and with her right hand, swung the handbag, catching Bill squarely across the face. Cowboy stepped out of the way to allow Bill to splay out onto the tarmac like a squid. The score was even.

Things progressed, as they do with COPD, so that eventually, Cowboy was unable to breathe without round-the-clock oxygen, as well as Xanax to reduce the symptoms of anxiety that came with difficulty in breathing. During this period, he decided to grow a marijuana plant. This was during Nancy Reagan's War on Drugs, and there were helicopters constantly flying over Washington County, looking for clandestine cannabis operations. He started a seedling in his one sunny window, and with great satisfaction, watched it flourish to a height of two and a half feet. From its position in that window, facing the street, it could be seen by any passerby turning around in Cowboy's cul-de-sac. Someone did see it, and decided they had to report it. Did they know Cowboy? He could barely breathe, much less smoke.

The next day, a county sheriff showed up knocking, and Terry let him in. Cowboy welcomed the uniformed peace officer into his home, as he did all company, and offered him a seat and a cup of coffee. The sheriff took in Cowboy's condition, then spoke in an apologetic tone.

"I guess someone called that in," he began, pointing to the healthy, flowering pot plant, "and that's why they sent me out." The officer could see the absurdity of what he was going to have to do and said so. "I'm awful sorry to have to take this," he said, "but the law's the law." Cowboy put up no fuss. He knew it was illegal. It had already given him great joy to grow it to this stage, seeing how it produced new leaves every time he suckered it. The sheriff apologized once more before leaving, thanked Cowboy for the coffee, and walked out to his cruiser with the plant. Terry patted Cowboy's shoulders, saying, "What a bunch of BS!" Cowboy only replied, "He was just doing his job."

The story has a footnote. Finn, known by all for his talents and resourcefulness, happened to be on his way to the dump with a load of construction debris. He was sitting at the stop sign in town in front of the Pine Tree Store when the sheriff went by, headed out the Grand Lake Road. Finn fell in behind him, but not too closely, since his plates were six years out of date. When the cruiser was just about at the entrance to the landfill, Finn saw something go flying out the passenger window of the cruiser and land in the ditch. Captivated by curiosity, he decided not to let the sheriff see him stop but waited until he'd dropped off his load at the dump to come back.

Imagine his surprise when Finn, no stranger to cannabis, picked up the fully flowered pot plant already showing buds. It was the perfect excuse to inaugurate his own clandestine cannabis operation, hiding in plain sight behind his house. Nancy Reagan suffered a setback that day, and when the telephone grapevine brought the news to Cowboy that the plant had been retrieved and was alive and thriving, he knew he had some news that would make Terry's day.

As his health declined, and with it his beloved hobbies, there remained many hours of the day to fill. Feeding critters filled that gap. For this, Cowboy, with Terry's help, requisitioned an area of the kitchen as a scullery to keep inventory for this purpose. Fish carcasses that I was able to bring back from fishing trips were frozen, then thawed out piecemeal, to keep the large family of raccoons that visited every night happy. For bears, Terry had to add chocolate-covered donut holes to her grocery list. Under Cowboy's direction, she pounded finishing nails into hemlock trees behind Cowboy's house, about chest high. She then pushed a donut hole onto each one of these nails. Within a few nights, they came. First one, then two, then three. One got so used to this food source that he began sleeping under a cantilevered section of the house, waiting for nightfall.

The most rewarding of all of Cowboy's feeding stations was his bird feeder, and not only because he loved watching the many varieties of birds coming to it. A war of wits between Cowboy and one particularly tenacious red squirrel kept him up nights, scheming and devising. By this time, Cowboy was spending as much time in his hospital bed as in his wheelchair. He had the bed situated alongside the partition between the living room and the kitchen, looking out the double-sash window facing the street. Here again, Terry followed his blueprint: She dug a hole just below what would be the frost line in winter and stuck a length of PVC pipe into it. The pipe was four inches in diameter. On top of it, she secured a birdhouse with feeding trays, using hose clamps, screws, and glue. About a foot below the feeder, she mounted a lampshade-shaped piece of sheet metal. This would prevent squirrels from climbing the pipe, since they would be unable to get around this broad obstruction. Before this, Cowboy had tried wheel bearing grease on the PVC pipe, but as it aged, his wily "limb rat" was able to get past the coagulated grease.

The lampshade idea worked like a charm. Cowboy loved watching his adversary study his creation from below while birds were swarming like bees to the feeder. The squirrel looked positively disconsolate. But he studied a little harder. Within a few days, as Cowboy was watching the robust activity at his feeder, which was costing him a forty-pound bag of black oil sunflower seed each week, a red squirrel landed on the roof of the feeder as if it had fallen from a plane. With a whittled cane stick he kept beside the bed, Cowboy reached over and tapped the window, frightening the intruder, who then jumped off. But in less than an hour, he was back. Cowboy bristled. Terry had left for the day, which meant he'd have to wait until the next day before he could take any action. He had all night to think.

When Terry came to work the next day, she learned that there was a more pressing concern than washing dishes, fluffing up the bed, or making lunch. Cowboy posted her in his garage across the yard from the house. From there, she could look out the garage window and see the feeder. He needed to know where the squirrel was coming from when he landed on the feeder. Terry got through a couple cups of coffee and several cigarettes before she saw it. Out of nowhere, a red squirrel appeared on the roof of Cowboy's house. There were some spruce trees within jumping distance of the house, so she reasoned that had to be how he got there. After what looked to her like a long deliberation, the red squirrel made a running start, flew off the roof, and landed firmly on the feeder. It was just within its longest jumping range

Cowboy slapped his knee when he heard the news. "That son-of-a-gun!" he said, smiling broadly. Terry knew him well enough by now that she didn't expect a plan right away. He would bring the same consideration to this problem that he had brought to his wool tapestries and to his music library.

It was too late in the year to dig up the PVC pipe and move the feeder farther away from the house. There was already frost in the ground. That meant devising a plan to convince the "chicken of the tree" that jumping onto the feeder was a really bad idea. Cowboy transferred himself to his wheelchair and turned up his concentrator to temporarily provide him with more oxygen. From a kitchen drawer full of odds and ends, he retrieved two extension cords, one six feet long, and one twelve, and a roll of duct tape. He returned to the coffee table next to his hospital bed and picked up his Barlow knife. He kept a sharpening stone on the table too, and he passed the blade across it twice on each side. With the blade, he easily cut off the female end of the twelve-foot extension. Then he split the two insulated wires apart, down to about six inches below where the plug had been. Carefully, he shaved back the insulation on these two leads, leaving half an inch of bare wire at the end of each.

When Terry arrived, she found him in his bed with his oxygen concentrator at its usual setting and everything else looking normal except that Cowboy wore a wide, mischievous grin.

"I smell trouble," she said as she went into the kitchen to make a pot of coffee.

"Good nose," Cowboy replied. As they shared their traditional first cup of coffee together, he laid out his plan. Right next to his bed on the partition wall was an electrical outlet. He'd already plugged in the male end of the six-foot extension there. The male end of the twelve-foot extension was plugged into the female end of the six-footer. He proudly held up the bare wires at the end of the twelve-footer and detailed the rest of his plan to Terry.

Being up on a step ladder with a staple gun and doing some very detailed duct-taping had Terry wondering whether she'd seen any of this in her job description when she'd applied to be Cowboy's caregiver. Before coming down, she filled the feeder to the brim with black oil sunflower.

For his part, Cowboy was as happy as he'd been in ages watching her, step by step, as she brought his plan to life. She'd executed all of it perfectly, all of the cord firmly secured to the pipe and to the roof, leaving only the two bare leads sticking up slightly. The other end of this cord came up to the double sash window, where it plugged into the six-foot cord, the male end of which Cowboy held in his hand beside the bed. When she came in and sat down, Cowboy held up the plug and said, "I'm gonna wait till his front paws are on one lead and his balls are on the other."

Terry, long past the point of blushing at Cowboy's language, smiled. "I hope I'm not here to see that." She told me later that, in her work as a caregiver, she often noticed with old men that, toward the end of their lives, the little boy inside them seemed to come out to play more often.

Terry got her wish. She was not there when it happened. I showed up only hours after Cowboy's plot struck pay dirt. The squirrel came, as Cowboy knew he would, but he was acting very cautious once he landed on the feeder, as if he recognized that something was different. Nevertheless, he began to hang upside down from the roof, getting food out of the tray below as he usually did. After eating enough to satisfy him and then stuffing his cheeks with even more, he came back up on the roof to eat. He remained skittish, as all squirrels are, moving around from place to place, keeping an eye out in all directions—all directions except down. Cowboy, watching intently, had the plug in his hand, only inches away from the outlet. He sat in the quiet. There was nothing on his TV or radio that could match this for excitement. When finally he was sure the rodent had settled into the perfect position, he thrust in the plug.

"Call me a liar if you want," he chuckled, still giddy while recounting his victory to me. "When the juice hit that critter, he went straight up and never did come down." At this, I went outside and looked around. I checked every place close to the feeder and then walked circles farther away. No sign. When I came back in shaking my head, he said, "He's up there with Sputnik," Sputnik being the most recent satellite Cowboy could remember.

After his long, slow decline, the end came quickly. In his usual mischievous manner, he looked up at me from his hospital bed in the skilled wing and said, "Stop the world, I want to get off." From then on, he stopped eating. No matter the appeals from the nursing staff or doctors, he replied with a polite "No thank you." Still, his body held out for almost thirty days on nothing but a sip of water now and then, just to "wet his whistle," as he would say. At one point he told me he had no fear at all, though all his life he'd thought he'd be afraid. He knew what he was doing and why. It looked to me like he was defending his choice to move on to the nurses and doctors.

Cowboy knew he had my blessing and my permission, and so, when my phone rang one morning at 6:00 a.m. and I saw that it was the hospital calling, I knew. I knew that my friend, who had captained his destiny to the last minute, was gone. After leaving the hospital that morning, I went and sat in his house with the remaining rugs, the music library, and his hospital bed, all made up as if he'd be returning any minute. I looked through one of the classic country cases, chose "I'm Movin' On," by Hank Snow, and slipped it into his cassette player. As the Singing Ranger rode "that big eight-wheeler" and the departing engine blew its whistle, I let my grief roll over me like the train Hank Snow was riding to get away from his troubles. When it was finished, I called Terry. I told her what Cowboy had asked me to do, and she agreed that we should choose a beautiful summer day to do it.

That day came in August. We met at Cowboy's house, then set out in my truck, hauling my Grand Laker behind. We put in at the state boat launch on West Grand Lake, near the lake's outlet. A slight breeze raised only a riffle on the surface as we proceeded at trolling speed. I took the route Cowboy would've taken as a young man with his stepfather, Harley Fitch, heading to the Oxbrook Camp at the mouth of Oxbrook. Terry clutched the box given to me by the Belfast Crematorium. I was blindsided when the man handing it over to me went into a military salute after I took it. Then he said, "On behalf of the U.S. Army Air Corps, we thank him for his service to his country." At that, Hank's train rolled over me a second time.

After the eight-mile crossing, we pulled up at the cribworks dock that had been in front of the Oxbrook Camp for decades. It was full of twists and undulations from years of ice movement, but still serviceable. The last time I'd been to the site was with Cowboy, just before he took up the wheelchair as his new means of getting around. That day, he sat in the tall grass growing around the camp among colorful wildflowers and stared at the glass-calm lake. His boyhood dreams still lived there, and he'd come for a visit with them.

The trail alongside Oxbrook leading to Lower Oxbrook Lake was still discernible but littered with deadfalls and blowdowns. It was the trail Harley had used when guiding sports up to his camp on Upper Oxbrook Lake in the 1930s, '40s, and '50s. In those days, Oxbrook itself was a bountiful brook trout fishery where Cowboy and his pal Bill spent countless hours.

After walking about a hundred yards, Terry and I both saw the same thing at the same time: a ledge in the stream forming a beautiful waterfall. The water cascaded down into a deep hole where it swirled, then bubbled up. A likely place for trout to lie. It was a hot summer day, and the water was surprisingly cold when, holding hands, we stepped along the ledge. Terry had been the best caregiver I could ever have imagined. I thanked her for that, and that's when her grief went under the big eight-wheeler too. We hugged, opened the box, and watched the Old Cowboy's ashes eddy and circle playfully before finally reaching the tail of the pool and being carried away.

2

The Mighty Finn

Finn has never been able to gain a pound. His weight and waist size have remained the same since he was sixteen. His metabolism has to be that of a titmouse. Watching him can make the most ambitious person feel like a slacker. Most photographs of him are blurry because he was on the go when the picture was taken, just like he is all the rest of the time.

Finn has been around for as long as anyone can remember, and although he isn't from here, no one still alive can seem to remember exactly when he arrived. One day, they say, it just seemed like he'd been here all along. That's the kind of personality Finn has. After you get to know him, you feel like you've known him all your life.

Since everyone around here has to have some identifying handle, the handle Finn got tagged with was "handyman," though anyone familiar with his skills would say that this sells him short. Is a man who can gather stones from roadsides and lake shores by the ton, truck them to a remote camp, and build a twelve-foot-wide fireplace and chimney with decorative sconces and ventilator ductwork a handyman? What about a man who can dream up a deep-water excavator built off the prow of a pontoon boat with pulleys and hooks that can move Volkswagen-sized boulders out of the way to make a channel? Is that a handyman? Only if it was handymen who built the Roman Colosseum and the Mayan temples.

In tiny, far-flung places like this one, it would do no good to brag about the kind of talent Finn has, since everyone already knows everything about you. If you tried it and your conceit rubbed someone wrong, they could easily produce something about you to counterbalance your big-headedness. Finn, like many other locals of exceptional virtuosity with their hands, simply goes about his business, content to let time and posterity judge the fruits of his labor.

In places like Chappaquiddick, Massachusetts, or the Hamptons on Long Island, Finn would be a millionaire many times over. He'd have a years-long waiting list of people hiring him to build their tall ship cupola, or their outdoor marble bar with sea turtle barstools, or their Moby Dick weather vane made of moose bone. He could do it all. And to do it all, he'd have to suffer summer people in Top-Siders and golf shirts, holding Manhattans in their delicate hands, talking him up to their socialite friends; and for Finn, well, that ship will simply never sail.

In contrast to that unsettling image, Finn is more comfortable on Beatrice's roof in blackfly season, repairing the leak that had her hobbling around the house emptying buckets all winter. The widow was short of funds to pay for the repairs, and rather than embarrass her, Finn accepted a bag of Doritos for the job, eating them right in front of her, which pleased Beatrice to no end. And if he didn't exactly want word to get out that he'd done that, it was pointless. Everyone already knew that, where his business acumen was deficient, his humanity was not.

Finn's lanky frame seemed capable of almost unnatural movement. This might have been due to a unique body design rarely encountered in Homo sapiens. Even as a young man, Finn wore his pants pulled up high, not because he was practicing being an old man, but because that's where his waist was. Once, at a town funeral in the local Congregational church, Finn showed up in a suit that drew more attention than the open casket up front. He was all pants. The necktie tucked into them was no more than six inches long. Finn was three-fifths legs and two-fifths torso, stretched over a frame that seemed perfectly suited for walking on plowed ground. Consequently, he could step effortlessly over objects in front of him, while his upper body remained motionless. To hunt with him was to witness a new animal in the woods, more dexterous than any deer. He walked across blowdowns, boulders, and deadfalls the way most of us walk on a sidewalk. His upper body would remain on an even plane, his rifle held against his chest in the port arms position.

If, from these accounts, you have begun to form a picture of Finn as an anomaly of nature, you would rightfully expect that such a man would have quirks. Idiosyncrasies. And there, you wouldn't be disappointed. As already hinted, he was beloved by some of the widows in town, shut-ins whose visitors included mostly other widows. For a man to drop by for them to feed, bake for, listen to, and be heard by was an indulgence these widows would blush to confess. And yet, they all loved to see him coming. The lack of a man around the house to check the furnace or clean the gutters or fix the faucet made Finn's company a valuable commodity. Flo, the widow of a lifelong trout fisherman, suddenly had to get used to a diet devoid of trout, something she'd grown very fond of. When fiddlehead season rolled around and swarms of blackflies could blot out the sun, her feelings of emptiness and dearth would redouble. Around that time, Finn would show up with both eyes swollen shut. His neck and head would be proud with angry, overlapping welts, and his pants would be soaking wet all the way up to his sternum, which is saying something in his case. But in his hand would be a creel which he would set down on Flo's kitchen table. When she came close to look, she could smell the muck on him from the beaver dams he'd scaled and the bushwhacking he'd done to get to prime, wild trout pools. When he threw back the flap on the creel, Flo would see five beautifully speckled brook trout lying in moss, and her hands would go up to her mouth.

Finn would not leave her with the job of cleaning the trout. Flo's husband had seen to that all their life together, and now Finn would do the honors while she set a warm cruller and a hot cup of coffee in front of him. Before leaving, he'd accept Flo's invitation to return for dinner that evening, after he'd had a chance to clean up.

As far as Finn's quirks went, visiting widows did not rise to the level of oddness that some of his others did. For the longest time, Finn had it in his head that one of the things he wanted to accomplish in life was to ride a moose. He shared this with me and others close to him, but was never rewarded with even the tiniest shred of encouragement, since none of us could even remotely see this as a good idea. Yes, a moose is horse-like in stature, but the likeness ends there. They are exceedingly retiring animals, often galled or offended by human scent or presence. To attempt to ride one, under any circumstances, would be to give deep trouble a formal invitation.

Years passed. His objective was never far from his thoughts. When an opportunity arose, he didn't want to be caught off guard. He described one close call to me. Once, floating down Grand Lake Brook in a double-end canoe, a five hundred-pound cow moose slipped into the stream just ahead of Finn. She apparently hadn't seen or heard him, but when he took several furious paddle strokes to catch up to her, she did. His idea was to pull up parallel to her, stand up, leap, and straddle her while she was still swimming. The problem was that the stream in that section was only fifteen feet wide. By the time he paddled up alongside the mammoth, her front hooves had already found a footing. Lurching up, she easily capsized the canoe just as Finn stood up. Luck itself was another of Finn's quirks. His record of falling from scaffolding, trees, and roofs and walking away unscathed was legend in this town. Once again, Finn came through this test without a scratch to show for it. Nor was he thwarted from his mission. He did say that the moose, once safely up on the bank, took a moment to stare at him, which, he said, made him feel slightly embarrassed. Analyzing this incident afterward, he could see the flaws. If it happened again, it would have to be in a wider, deeper stream, or preferably in a lake.

Then, the following year—the year he was trucking rocks out to the camp where he was building the fireplace that will be there a hundred years from now—he drove up on a moose standing in the middle of the gravel road. Stalemates in this situation are common. Standoffs occur when a vehicle stops and the staring contest begins. In this period, the moose is making up its mind. That mind is reputedly housed in a walnut-sized brain, providing all the more reason for caution.

This specimen was a bull that would've dressed out in the 850 to 900-pound range, according to Finn. Except that it wasn't dressed out. That would mean it was dead. This bull, with all of its organs and viscera intact, probably weighed 1100 pounds. It was September, so its antlers had reached their maximum growth, and this one had a spread of close to sixty inches. Finn knows that because, very soon, he'd have a reason for measuring the spread.

Moose antlers, especially the highly sought-after ones, have broad palms, as well as points, or tines, growing out of the palms. A set of majestic headgear like that in front of Finn's truck can weigh up to forty pounds. The disposition of an already irritable bull carrying this kind of weight on its head should be given great heed by anyone who comes close. The organization that has been scoring these horns since 1887 is the Boone and Crockett Club, a conservation group with very strict rules. All Finn could say after this encounter was that this bull would surely have impressed Boone and Crockett.

Instead of putting his Dodge Ram truck into reverse and slowly backing away from danger, as anyone else would have done, Finn put the Dodge in forward. The moose stood its ground. Inch by inch, Finn crept closer. Finally, at about the twenty-foot mark, the bull turned its whole body toward the truck. Finn paused, then advanced another foot or so. The moose answered with a step. This was repeated several more times, until Finn was looking into the bull's eyes through his windshield.

Then the staring contest was over. Without warning, the bull lowered his head and locked the tines of his broad antlers into the front bumper of Finn's Ram truck, a set of horns to either side of the license plate. Then it began to rock the truck violently from side to side on its shock absorbers. This was it! The moment Finn had dreamed of. It seemed now as if the moose's antlers were stuck in the bumper, which meant he was stationary. Finn bailed from his pickup and tried a Roy Rogers-style running side mount, swinging his prodigious lower limbs as high as he could while the moose was still rocking and rolling the truck. Here again, there was a problem Finn had failed to calculate. A fully-grown adult moose can be nearly seven feet tall at the shoulder! That's less a high jump than a pole vault. Whether this bull was fully grown or not, it was tall enough that Finn's attempt was bollixed, and he fell in a heap under the beast. Unharmed as usual, he was gathering himself up for another go when one side of the moose's horns came unhooked from the bumper. In the split second that it took for Finn to think, "Uh oh," the other side was free. Later, Finn measured the width of his truck. It was sixty inches from one end of the front bumper to the other, and these moose horns encompassed all of it.

The moose turned to see Finn on the ground beside him, and when Finn looked into his eyes, he saw his own mortality. He rolled out of the way to miss a kick from one of the bull's hind legs, and quickly came to his feet. The moose swung its head, trying to knock Finn over with his horns, but Finn was already running. His legs might have been long, but the bull's were too, and the bull had four of them. He quickly realized that, on the straightaway, he had no chance. By the time he picked a spot to jump over the ditch and into the thick woods, he felt the breath of the bull on his back. Finn's sudden leap over the gulley must have flummoxed the moose, because he kept running for another fifty feet before stopping. This was Finn's chance to sprint back to the still-running truck, all of which the bull observed without moving.

Working on his fireplace later that day, Finn was in a reflective mood. He was beginning to think that his dream of mounting a moose for the ride of a lifetime had some flaws.

No portrait of Finn would be complete without a black lab sitting next to him. They were inseparable. As soon as Finn pulled up to the Pine Tree Store and got out, the lab moved into the driver's seat as if he'd driven Finn there. If Finn was on a roof, the lab was on the ground watching him. At any jobsite, the dog took up a position close to the work, looking as though, if he were asked to pass a hammer, he gladly would. The only trips he wasn't allowed to go on were moose and deer hunting trips, since hunting big game in Maine with dogs is illegal. Ice fishing was another story. The pads under the lab's paws had to be impervious to cold, for he'd stay out on the ice with Finn for whole days at a time. If Finn was spending the night in the ice shack, the dog would nestle on the bench beside him, giving off almost as much warmth as the tiny propane heater.

Many visitors to the area are curious as to why anyone would want to be out on a frozen lake overnight, listening to the wind howl and the ice quake underfoot. The simple answer is cusk. Admittedly a bit of an eerie creature, it is best fished for at night, when it is most active. Anglers come from great distances to stay in a six-by-eight-foot shack for a week in order to catch a few cusk. If they adhere to the law book, they either stay up all night, or set an alarm to go off every hour, since the law requires you to check your lines that often. The payoff, according to cusk connoisseurs, is the most delectable meat found on any freshwater fish anywhere. Some chunk it into scallop-shaped cubes and deep-fry them in a batter. Others dice up the sweet, white meat for fish chowders and dare anyone to say it isn't better than haddock.

Finn too was a fan of cusk. In February, when the pack basket was full and the ice augur was packed with it into the back of the truck, the dog knew what was up. Treats were in store for him on these outings, when exotic smells and cooked fish spiced up his usual diet.

The ice had come in late that year. Finn could remember years when it was safe to ice skate on Thanksgiving. Those days are gone. Christmas and even New Year's are apt to see open water, even if some of the coves are buttoned up with ice by then. By opening day, February 1, the Warden Service was urging caution on the larger lakes. Finn heard the reports, but his favorite destination was a cove where he'd discovered good cusk fishing several years before. There would be no need to wander out into the middle of the lake. There was also no need to get going too early, since the cusk don't start biting until darkness sets in.

After a full day's work, Finn packed up, and by the time he got everything squared away at home and set out, it was 8:00 p.m. Deep snows had not arrived yet, and by the time he reached the lake, he could see that he'd have to put the truck into four-wheel drive to keep from skidding sideways on the glare ice. Even so, braking would be difficult, so it was best to go slow. From the west shore of West Grand Lake, he could look east and see the light of a small colony of ice shacks plugged in between Munson Island and Bonny Brook. It was a new precinct of Grand Lake Stream that popped up there every February. These anglers were after whitefish, and after the weather forecast that Finn had just heard on the truck radio, he knew tomorrow would be a busy day in the neighborhood.

When Munson Island slipped away to his right, he knew he was crossing over a couple of rock shoals no more than two feet under the ice in some places. If his truck punched through right there, he could "stand up and drink," as the old-timers used to say. Ice reports had been decent, though, so Finn felt reasonably good about the ice under him. When he traveled another mile

35

and reached Big Mayberry Cove, he looked east again and saw a lone light, seemingly in the middle of the lake. This would be somebody's ice shack, set out on an area known as the Twin Sisters. I'd flown over them by floatplane in the summer and seen them appearing as two sunken islands of roughly the same size, perhaps a quarter of an acre each. Salmon, togue, and whitefish gathered there in the winter for the schools of smelts that flourished in the area. But it was also one of the hotspots for cusk, known to a few of those unstoppable nocturnal fishermen. Someone was out there, all right, probably pulling up one of those alien-looking fish this very minute, Finn mused.

Even with no moon and a low fog settling over the lake, he could make out Norway Point up ahead on his left. A tiny island separated from the mainland by only fifty feet, Norway Point had a storybook log camp set amongst its Norway pines. Finn had always admired the place with its red trim, built decades ago by Sonny Sprague. He'd seen its owners wading out to the island over the sand bar connecting it to shore. In August, the bar was not much more than ankle-deep.

Around that point was Finn's destination: Farm Cove. Of all the places on the vast lake, it had always been one of his favorites. Even the lab stood up on the seat and perked up his ears after they'd rounded the point. The problem was that there was now a disorienting fog blocking Finn's view in any direction. Fog is one of the weather phenomena most feared by winter fishermen. If you happen to be caught without a compass or GPS in a winter pea soup, you may as well be the Ancient Mariner, minus an albatross. The disorientation will prevent you from going in a straight line to any point, possibly condemning you to go around in circles until you run out of fuel or energy, or until the fog lifts. Finn had heard all of the same local tales that I had about some of those lost souls who met their death in just such a fog. The same sort of panic sets in under those conditions as that which a lost hunter experiences when he realizes he recognizes nothing around him and has no idea which way to go.

The one thing Finn wasn't thinking about was open water. After all, why would there be any in February, in a cove that was usually deemed safe before other areas of the lake? But there, up ahead, he could make out something that looked different, darker than what his headlights had been illuminating all the way up the lake. He allowed himself to get a little closer before the thought of what it might be struck him like an electric shock. That's when Finn stood on the brakes. Had his realization not been so abrupt, he might have pumped them instead and slowly come to a halt. Now, his wheels locked up, sending him forward at an even faster clip. In seconds flat, an open maw appeared before him, and the shale ice under the truck's front tires gave way. A vice grip of shock and fear closed Finn's throat as the vehicle broke through and plunged into the lake, floating only briefly before heading down, front first, since all the weight was under the hood.

If somebody survives calamities like this one, it's always the oddest things that they remember afterward. For Finn, it was how long the lights of the dashboard stayed on, even after the truck was totally submerged. He thought for sure that water would short out every electrical connection and cast him into darkness right away. Not so. When the truck's front wheels hit bottom and the rear of the truck followed, those dash lights were still on.

Of all the things that might save your life in situations like the one Finn was now in, it's a chemical that's most likely to do it. That chemical is adrenalin. Finn's admirable creativity was no good to him now. Nor was his analytical mind or his engineering skills. Those required reflection, contemplation. The fight-or-flight mechanism was in charge now, and that meant rapid-fire action. The water pressure pushing against the door made it impossible to open. Had his truck had power windows, he might not have been able to get out, but Finn preferred roll-down windows. The water rushed in as the black lab whimpered and cowered on the seat next to him. Finn grabbed him firmly by the collar, waited until the cab was half full of water, then had to let go of the dog to climb out the window. When he reached back in with the help of the still-lit dashboard, the dog moved away. The water was now up to his neck. Finn yelled and screamed at him. The lab only resisted more. Finally, with his own breath at stake, he inhaled deeply and began swimming upward, stroke by stroke, unable to discern how deep it was where he went down. When at last he broke through the surface, he gasped desperately for air. And now, here was another moment Finn would remember long afterward: Out of all that impenetrable darkness, Finn saw one dim light shimmering some distance away. But his thoughts were below him. The dog. Finn took as big a breath as his lungs could hold and dove back down.

I have asked myself many times, who do I know, other than Finn, who would do that? And then I always remember that Finn was in Khe Sanh during the Vietnam war. It was one of the longest and costliest sieges of that dark era, and for Finn, it meant being trapped in a valley of death for seventy-seven days, losing friends and wondering which of those days would be his last. After surviving that siege, Finn was given service medals, as if they could compensate for the lifelong survivor's guilt and PTSD that would accompany him for the rest of his days. These consequences of his heroic soldiering, of course, were faltering relationships and battles with substance abuse which would ultimately consign him to the life of a loner; but he had one constant companion who understood him and accepted him as he was—that dog that was trapped in his truck.

Had it not been for the dash lights shining like a beacon from the bottom of the lake, Finn might not have been able to find the truck. It was, nevertheless, too late. The cab had filled with water and the dog had drowned, paralyzed in panic on the front seat. The realization released an air bubble of raw emotion from Finn's lungs, and now he had to bolt to the surface to save himself. But that was still very much in question. Hypothermia was already taking hold as Finn thrashed his arms, breaking the thin ice where the truck had gone through. He kicked and swam clumsily to find ice that would not break under his fists. Finally, when he slammed down both hands, the ice held. He'd reached ice that was strong enough just as his own strength was nearly played out. But then, each time he tried to pull himself up, kicking his feet, his grip gave way and he slipped back in.

The third thing that he'd always remember afterward happened next. He suddenly recalled that, earlier that day, he'd been at a camp where he was caretaker, fixing the dock, which had been destroyed the previous winter by ice. It is unlawful to leave docks in the lake over the winter unless they were "grandfathered in" by virtue of being older than the regulation. This one was. It was the classic dock design of the previous century. A series of cribworks filled with rocks formed a foundation onto which decking could be nailed. When ice damages such things, it does so on the way out, not on the way in, as many might think. When the ice goes out in the spring, it wrenches and pulls and is capable of upending giant boulders in the lake. In this case, it had twisted the cribworks out of alignment so that Finn had to tear up all the decking and practically start over.

And that's what Finn remembered—the galvanized twenty-penny nails he'd stuffed in his shirt pockets while he was nailing down the new decking. Keeping himself afloat by kicking both feet as hard as he could, he reached into each shirt pocket and pulled out a nail. Clasping them in his palms, he drove them into the ice and pulled himself out. He knew, from legend and lore, and from the stories that are passed down about going through the ice, that you do not stand up after pulling yourself out of the lake. If you do, you will most likely plunge right back through. Still using the nails, Finn pulled himself along, supine, until he felt himself to be at a safe distance from the open water. Then, he stood up, dripping and frozen.

But now what? Uncontrollable shivering set in, indicating stage two hypothermia. Minutes mattered, but he was miles from anywhere and no way to get there. And then, miraculously, there it was again—that one light, the one he'd seen when he'd first surfaced, before diving back down for the dog. Could it be a mirage? The wishful creation of a brain's circuitry just before blinking out? No matter. Finn made for it, one sliding step after another, as if he were cross country skiing. He fell twice, but the work of walking seemed to alleviate the shivering slightly. He even felt himself picking up speed as he realized the light was larger now, closer. He called out, "Hey! Hello! Anybody?"

The door of the ice shack opened. A man in skivvies stood there. Two ATVs were parked alongside the shack. Another man appeared, stepping out onto the ice with a lantern. When he saw Finn, he said, "Jesus!" and grabbed him. He called to his companion, and they both helped Finn into the shack, where he collapsed on the floor.

When Finn awoke, he was naked but wrapped in a blanket, sitting on the floor next to the woodstove. The men who had taken him in were from New Hampshire, up for a long weekend for a chance at some cusk, togue, or whitefish, they said. Finn felt his insides thawing, and eventually his hands and toes, too. He told them what had happened, about the truck and the dog. "Oh man, that's hard," one of them said. They told Finn he'd slept fitfully for a few hours while they had his clothes drying on nails behind the stove. When daylight came, Finn dressed in his dry clothes, and they gave him coffee, two fried eggs, and toast. They told him they needed to pick up some things in town anyway, which he doubted, so it would be no trouble to drop him off. Finn had nothing to give them, only heartfelt handshakes and thanks.

Once again, Finn had walked away from something that could easily have claimed his life, and for several weeks after, he wondered whether he wished it had. But the widows, Finn's fan club, went to work, because there's always another dog—not the same dog, and certainly not one that knows you as well, but those things can come in time. They busied themselves on their phones, calling shelters, veterinary offices, breeders, and each other. They would repay Finn's kindnesses, his visits, his company, his appreciation of their baking gifts, and his handyman work around their houses for nothing more than a bag of chips or an apple crisp. It was true that, since the accident, his visits had fallen off. When seen around town, he had a downcast appearance, his head and shoulders more slumped than usual.

Then, a breakthrough. A black lab pup had been born across the border in St. Stephen, New Brunswick. It was the veterinarian there who passed along the information about the litter to one member of the widow posse, who immediately rallied the others. The pup wasn't free, far from it, and at $250, it was a sum none of them could come up with on their own. But old ladies, as everyone knows, have stashes and caches and slush funds. They're in cookie jars, jewelry boxes, and bibles. There were five widows, and they were each able to manage fifty dollars. When one of their daughters picked up the pup at ten weeks old, she brought him around to all five for their lavish approval. None of them had been so animated in ages. Next came the scheme to get Finn out of himself, out of his dark night of the soul. It would take the right bait to lure him.

Mice. That was it! Mary had a mice problem. They were eating her out of house and home and keeping her up nights. She didn't even have to lie; it was all true, and she'd tried everything she knew. Normally, she'd wait for Finn to visit, but he was lying low since the lake incident, so she called.

When Finn came in, dark-eyed and with several days of stubble on his face, the smell of cinnamon sticky buns permeated the whole house. Fresh coffee, brewed in the percolator, was ready. Finn had no idea what was in the offing, so he listened while Mary explained her problem. The kind of poison they sell now in those little cubes doesn't work as well as the old kind that came in granular form. "They're wise to it," she told him. After killing a couple of them in a conventional mousetrap, the others started avoiding it, no matter what she put in there. She swore that every time one died, twelve came to its funeral.

Finn politely excused himself. He went out to his truck bed and retrieved a five-gallon drywall compound pail. When he came back, he asked Mary if he could go into the shop. That was where her late husband made ash canoe seats for Grand Laker canoes. Finn found what he was looking for—a half-inch dowel, which was used to hinge the seats so that they could fold down. With Mary looking on, he filled the bottom of the pail with about four inches of water, then asked if she had any peanut butter. She produced some, and Finn pasted it generously around the middle of the dowel, then laid it across the top of the pail. He then leaned a stick of kindling he'd found in the shop up to the rim of the pail. "You'll catch at least one mouse a night this way until they're either all dead or discouraged," he told her. Just then came a knock at the door.

The daughter who'd picked up the pup had driven the other four ladies over, along with the lab. Finn and Mary were seated at the kitchen table when Mary shouted, "Come in!" The ladies had powwowed on how best to go about this. They knew Finn. Anything ceremonious would be the wrong way to go. The best thing would be directness. Just hand over the dog and see what happened.

No heart is so broken or bereft as to be unreachable by a ten-week-old lab pup. Its love is unconditional, its healing powers unfathomable. Finn tried to defend himself, briefly, by fidgeting with his jacket zipper, then sipping coffee, and then taking a bite of cinnamon bun. But when the daughter sat down beside him, the pup jumped out of her arms and onto Finn's lap. Finn let it nuzzle him for a long moment before finally running his hand across its back. Hearing sniffles, he looked up to see Mary passing out tissues to everyone.

Finn is older now. His gait has slowed as his legs have bowed, but other than that, only one thing has changed. His death-defying adventurism is a thing of the past, perhaps owing to a sneaking suspicion that he may now be living his ninth life. This dog, too, jumps into the driver's seat of Finn's truck when it pulls up to the Pine Tree Store. And yes, it's the same truck. Finn, with help, had recovered his truck using a tree-length log tripod and skids, the way they'd done since vehicles first arrived in Grand Lake Stream and someone first managed to drown one. If ingenuity paid well, Grand Lake Stream would be full of millionaires.

This dog does one thing his predecessor couldn't. He has the uncanny ability to know where Finn is inside the house when he's outside it. There are three entrances, and no matter which one Finn goes to in order to let him in, he's there. He's tested this by walking to one door, seeing him there waiting, and then tiptoeing to another door, only to find him there too.

Time wounds all heels and heals all wounds, as the saying goes, but time sometimes needs help, and that help came to Finn in canine form. The pooch accompanies Finn to visit the two remaining widows of the five who conspired on his behalf. But now there are others, because in Grand Lake Stream, it's the women who are built to last. If Finn should ever decide to marry again, he'd have his pick from a willing list of widows over eighty who would welcome in matrimony a man who knows how to fix things, loves apple crisp, and is a good listener. So far, Finn seems happy enough with the hound.

3

Poor Farm

For some, Grand Lake Stream is the beginning of a dream; for others, it's the end of the line. For some, it's their first chance to truly be themselves; for others, it's a chance to be somebody entirely new.

For all the assaults it has suffered, Grand Lake Stream still has a heartbeat. The worldwide trend is moving from rural to urban; schools are shrinking, brick and mortars are being shuttered, and people are making their livings with their heads, not their hands. Even for all that, this little oasis stubbornly persists.

As the Native Americans living next door have shown us, the one thing that can't be taken away from a community is its oral history, provided there's even one person left to carry it on. That's all it takes for its heart to keep beating. It's true that a few books have been written about the area, including a history called *Hinckley Township; or, Grand Lake Stream Plantation, A Sketch*, which is an out-of-print collectible. But what really lives on are the stories, shared by guides with sports, remembered on the Liar's Bench in the Pine Tree Store, retold in remote camps in winter when the ash settles white and the lamps burn low. These are our lifeblood, these stories, starring the colorful characters that have populated this place since tannery times. That's when the population topped a thousand and news from across the world was brought in with shipments of hides to be tanned. The resulting melting pot of nationalities, heritages, and traditions was absorbed into Grand Lake Stream, where, eventually, almost everyone would owe their existence to transients who'd come from someplace else. The proud claim of being a native here rings hollow down the halls of history.

How could such a culture not produce one-of-a-kind characters? They wrote and recited limericks, sang songs they'd brought with them from foreign shores, and performed magic tricks to the delight of children. And there was always a clogger who could skip the light fandango across a sawdust floor.

Let's say you could interview one of Grand Lake Stream's older citizens, someone old enough to remember the aftermath of the tannery closing down. She'd likely remember Frank Ball's Store on Ball Hill, even before Paul Hoar built the Pine Tree Store, out of which he sold groceries, hardware, outdoor gear, and even insurance. She might repeat the standard story about Paul hiring a high school kid to work behind the counter when the busy salmon season opened in the spring. The boy was trying his best to do well at it so he could keep the job for the summer. But it was tough when some of the needier customers from "from away" came in, like the fellow who strode up to the counter one day demanding a "half head of lettuce." The boy knew his stock and politely replied that the Pine Tree Store only carried whole heads of lettuce.

"You must not have heard me, boy," said the determined customer, amping up his voice slightly. "So I'll say it again. I said I want half a head of lettuce."

"I'm sorry," the teen explained. "We only have whole heads of lettuce here." At this, the man went from determined to adamant, adding a few more decibels to his demand.

"Listen, boy," he said, so close now that his knees were pressing up against the counter. "I'm the customer, right?"

"Um, ah, rrrr...ight."

"And the customer's always right, right?"

"Um, right. Yessir."

"Well then, listen to me again. I want half a head of lettuce! Got it?" This time, he spoke so loudly that the other customers stopped shopping to take notice, embarrassing the boy. The last thing he wanted was to make a scene.

"I'll go check with my boss, then," he said, coming around the counter and heading to Paul's office in the back. On the way, he seethed, angrier with each step, his reddened face feeling like a pressure cooker. But, unbeknownst to the boy, the cantankerous customer followed him right up to the open door of Paul's office. The boy couldn't contain himself when he confronted his boss. He took a deep breath and said, "Some asshole out front wants a half a head of lettuce." But when he saw Paul's eyes looking over his shoulder, he quickly turned, saw the man, and said, "…and this gentleman right here would like to buy the other half." Paul was so impressed he hired the boy for the summer right on the spot.

By now, your voice-of-the-past hostess has finished brewing a pot of coffee and has set something baked down in front of you. She knows she's already got you hooked. She asks if you've ever heard of the Poor Farm. You say no, and watch the grin cross her face.

It was still standing only thirty years ago. To her, that's a few minutes ago. The people who ended up there might today be called indigents, but the town didn't treat them that way. They were simply without means or a place to live, and almost everyone in town had experienced that in some form or another. The Poor Farm, therefore, drew interesting folk from the margins of society, perhaps unable to navigate life in a conventional way. They did, however, know how to grow their own vegetables in the open space around the Poor Farm. And they could milk the cow, and collect the eggs, and butcher a deer or a moose. And so, in this way, the tenants of the Poor Farm, at any given time, were getting by. They could also be relied on to help when there was a fire, or when extra bodies were needed for moving a building or volunteering at the hatchery when it was fin-clipping time.

Sometimes, someone at the Poor Farm was able to make the transition into Grand Lake Stream itself by finding work and their own place to live. Jumpy was one such case. To the town's credit, no one here hung this handle on the poor sufferer of Tourette's syndrome, a condition which caused him to make sudden, unexpected movements and sometimes simultaneously shout expletives. Everyone around the Poor Farm had gotten used to him, and to these brief, unexpected fits. Jumpy would even laugh along with them if it produced a comical result, which it often did.

There was little comedy in Jumpy's past. The disease had wreaked havoc on his life. He was bullied as a child, and as a result his pent-up anger terrorized his twenties. This led him to alcoholism, barroom brawls, arrests, and even time in the slammer. But these stories, told around the woodstove on winter nights, were shocking to no one. Every single tenant had a past, and the Poor Farm was a place where they could freely talk about it and not be judged, perhaps for the first time in their life.

Now in his forties, Jumpy had learned how to live with his Tourette's as well as anyone could. This meant he no longer had to fight the world, no longer had to drink himself into a coma. With those things out of the way, he discovered that he loved to work. The trouble was, he now found himself in a place where jobs were about as scarce as coconut trees. For the first few years, he did everything he could, cleaning cabins in sporting lodges and odd-jobbing around the premises for the owners. He did a part-time stint at the salmon hatchery, cleaning the raceways when they were about to be populated with new fish. He even walked dogs for summer people, having learned that dogs got used to his malady far faster than humans.

The problem was that none of this work was steady. As the remedy for this chronic Grand Lake Stream condition, Jumpy decided to invent his own vocation. One day in April, while he was bringing trash to the landfill from one of the sporting lodges, he saw that someone had discarded a camper. It was about twenty feet long and still had air in the tires. True, it was not in great shape; it needed paint, trim, a roof, and windows, but Jumpy immediately saw it in a completely new light. It would become his "takeout," where he'd serve up hot dogs and hamburgers and other treats to hungry fishermen, as well as tourists traveling through. It was an idea that he didn't know had been brewing inside him until he saw the camper.

No one at the Poor Farm had a driver's license, including Jumpy. It could almost be said, at one point in time, that driver's licenses in Grand Lake Stream were optional. There was no law to speak of, except an occasional appearance by the district game warden, and checking driver's licenses was far from his top priority. Sometimes license plates from bygone years were still being used just to fill that rectangular space on the bumper. In short, no one asked or cared whether you were licensed or not. So when Jumpy asked the lodge owner for whom he was odd-jobbing if he could use the lodge pickup to tow a camper from the landfill to the Poor Farm, he readily agreed.

The arrival of Jumpy's camper at the Poor Farm was greeted in celebratory fashion. His fellow tenants assumed it meant that he was planning an elaborate cross-country adventure.

"No," Jumpy corrected them, just before having one of his episodes. "It's going to be—FUCK! SHIT!—my takeout." Jumpy took a deep breath, then laughed along with them at his unintended outburst. The next day, he set to work. Beside the narrow door on the side of the camper where there was one window, Jumpy ripped a larger hole to make a second. Over time the Poor Farm had compiled what almost passed for a workshop, with tools donated, found, or simply left behind by former residents. With a scissors jack Jumpy found in there, he jacked up the camper and made the changes he would need for a Frialator, including the holes and fittings for propane.

He ransacked the interior of bedding and furniture and replaced it all with counter space and cupboards. Over the space where the grill would be, he tore a hole in the ceiling for venting, and he soon found a ventilation fan, discarded by a sporting camp, at the dump. Doors were opening for Jumpy. The more the camper looked like his vision, the more his enthusiasm grew.

People came and went at the Poor Farm. It had always been that way, almost as if it functioned unintentionally as a halfway house, providing respite from whatever had gone before or a springboard for whatever was to come after. In that way, Rizzie turned up out of the blue one day from God-knows-where, but it was the unspoken custom at the Poor Farm not to question newcomers about their pasts. It would most likely come out in due time. As she got settled and got to know everybody, she told them she'd once had a summer job at a takeout in her hometown. Another door had just opened for Jumpy.

A rush of fishermen would soon arrive in Grand Lake Stream in late May. This propelled Jumpy into high gear. He filed his applications with the Board of Health, put in a warrant to the town to be allowed a site near the town dock for his takeout, and began to place his first orders for inventory. Rizzie chimed in on the items she'd known to sell best in summer. The list was short: hot dogs, hamburgers, french fries, and ice cream. You would also include, she said, pickles, coleslaw, and chips as sides for some of the orders. And it would help if you named things, rather than just letting people flounder over what they might want, which would hold things up, if there was a line.

"Like a Hot Dog Deluxe," she said, "with sauerkraut, onions, mustard, and relish. People will say, 'Oh, that sounds good,' and order it." Jumpy took a shine to Rizzie. She began to accompany him out to the camper, adding suggestions and touches here and there to make the operation more efficient.

"Have almost everything at arm's length," she counseled. "Trust me, you'll be glad you did." And that's exactly how Jumpy planned his "kitchen," which took up the entire camper. It was Rizzie's further suggestion to have an awning coming off of the side, and a picnic table or two under it. After hearing this, the first person Jumpy went to see was Guel Roberts, who ran the landfill.

In more than a trivial way, Guel Roberts was the gatekeeper of Grand Lake Stream. He was also a great judge of character. "You can tell a lot about people from their trash," he'd often say. That information, though sometimes highly personal, was safe with Guel. He brought an abiding affability to the most social gathering place in Grand Lake Stream. Everyone made their twice-weekly visits to drop off their trash, but more importantly, to visit with Guel, for he was the intersection of all gossip in Grand Lake Stream.

With only a couple of spells—arms akimbo, obscene utterances flying—Jumpy told Guel of his needs. Guel got the gist of it: Jumpy needed something that could be used as, or made into, an awning; and would he please get in touch the next time a lodge or camp owner discarded a picnic table? The dump was open two days a week, Wednesday and Saturday. This meeting took place on a Wednesday.

By Saturday, Jumpy was in clover. A summer person from Greenwich, Connecticut, who owned a compound eight miles uplake, kept a large seagoing vessel for those trips when the weather was up. He had arrived with a new canvas boat cover for this craft and dropped off the old one at the landfill. Then, in the section designated for wood, the skeletal remains of two picnic tables turned up. "It's your lucky day," was how Guel greeted Jumpy that Saturday morning.

On Monday, after Jumpy had picked up his permission at the town offices to park his takeout near the town dock, he was walking down the hallway when he met the first assessor coming from the other direction. Jumpy intended a polite salutation, but just as they were about to pass each other, an untimely spell came over him, causing him to appear to take a swing at the assessor. The assessor, who'd likewise been about to greet Jumpy and congratulate him on his new venture, feinted left, narrowly escaping the roundhouse that might have put him down for the count. Cognizant of Jumpy's ailment, or "tic" as some called it, he politely accepted the flood of apologies that followed, and both went on their way.

Rizzie's touches to the trailer were both practical and feminine. Jumpy took her up on her offer to make up the menu as well as the menu sign that would hang outside the takeout, next to the double windows. All around the margins, she painted wildflowers. She then calligraphed the menu, and her classy script made the prices seem that much more reasonable. Jumpy's takeout was unearthing talents she'd forgotten she had.

When Jumpy saw the finished product, he smiled. There it was, the Hot Dog Deluxe, looking quite deluxe indeed. And the "Landlocked Burger," named for our famous landlocked salmon fishing, was sure to score well, too. Rizzie had looked into ice cream on her own and decided that the only brand any self-respecting takeout could carry was Maine's own Gifford's Ice Cream, with both sugar and plain cones.

On Saturday, May 20, the Poor Farm folk gave Jumpy and Rizzie a send-off as Guel stopped through on his way to the landfill and hitched up the takeout camper to his pickup. Rizzie had completed the modifications to the canvas boat cover so that it was now a roll-up awning fitted between the braces that Jumpy had made. It and the refurbished picnic tables went into the back of the pickup.

Everything was in place before lunchtime. Jumpy and Rizzie placed the picnic tables carefully, with good views of the lake and boat launch. Rizzie covered both with red and white checkered plastic tablecloths, which had cost $1.49 each at the Princeton Variety. In time she hoped to replace those with linen. It was a sunny day, so the awning would serve only to provide shade. They both walked around and around the new business, and then walked over to the town dock to look back on it from that vantage.

"I guess we're partners," Jumpy said. No such discussion had passed between them up to that point. They'd just gotten on with the tasks at hand, but along the way, it had become obvious that they worked really well together.

"I guess we are," Rizzie agreed. "I wonder if they'd let us put a small sign up over there," she said, pointing to Grand Lake Lodge. It was the only sporting lodge from which you could see the takeout. Guests trailered up their own boats and docked them right in front of the lodge.

"I bet they would," Jumpy answered. He knew them, of course, having odd-jobbed and generally helped out around the place.

"Good. I'll make one up." They then discussed which other lodges might be willing to help them advertise. Jumpy explained the difference between lodges on the American plan and those on the housekeeping plan, the former providing all meals, the latter providing kitchens in guests' cabins. Grand Lake Lodge was of the latter type, and there were several others whose guests might like to know about a place where they could pick up a quick lunch.

At eleven thirty, Jumpy put the first hot dog and hamburger on the grill in preparation for a first customer. That turned out to be none other than the first assessor, who arrived wanting to show his support for a rare new business in town. As he stood back to read the ornately decorated menu, Rizzie quickly slipped the first batch of fries into the Frialator.

"I think I've got to go with the Hot Dog Deluxe Plate," said the assessor. For $5.75, the hot dog with sauerkraut, onions, mustard and relish, and a side of fries and coleslaw looked like a great deal. "Should I take a number?" he joked. The punch he'd ducked was still fresh in his mind.

"Be right up," Jumpy replied, having wanted to say those words ever since he first saw the camper at the landfill. A little nervous, he took special care to present a perfect plate. Rizzie had splurged on Chinet paper plates because of their sturdiness. Jumpy dressed the dog, careful not to crowd out the kraut by overloading the onions or overdoing the condiments. Rizzie positioned the fries and coleslaw so artistically that they both wished they'd taken a picture of it before letting it go. It was their first sale.

She handed it to Jumpy, but as she did, she saw the familiar contortion come across his face. It was too late. Already on his way to handing the plate through the window to the assessor, Jumpy's arms spasmed violently, the effect of which was to send the Deluxe Plate sailing out the window. Rizzie leaned over in time to see their first sale splatter off the assessor's shoulder and then fly past Lillian Fawcett's ear. She had apparently arrived on her bicycle, disappointed to discover that she would be the takeout's second customer, not its first, as she had hoped. Everyone froze for a moment, perhaps deliberating on the most appropriate reaction under the circumstances. But just then, several fishermen who had tied up at the town dock came over and got in line behind Lillian, as one of Grand Lake Stream's many roving dogs ate up the sacrificial Hot Dog Deluxe. Rizzie reached through the window, handing the assessor a fistful of napkins.

"That was our way of cutting the ribbon," she smiled. "Your Deluxe'll be right up," she added. She turned and gave Jumpy the first kiss she'd ever given him, then they both got busy—so busy that, before the day was out, Rizzie had to run up to the Pine Tree Store to buy several packages of hot dogs and buns. Sports coming off the lake to Grand Lake Lodge saw the activity and couldn't resist stopping over. Fishermen heading out for the afternoon stopped to pick up lunch and take it with them. Jumpy had no spells for the rest of that day.

The dinner crowd turned out to be more of an ice cream event, but by the end of the day, the takeout had gone through almost all of its inventory. Jumpy and Rizzie were sweaty, greasy, dirty, and tired, but the cash box was full. Giddy, they rolled up the awning and the plastic tablecloths, walked down to the town dock, and jumped in, forgetting that it was only May. They were out of the lake faster than they'd gone in.

On summer evenings, whoever happened to be living at the Poor Farm sat outside around a fire pit, faces aglow, watching the sparks fly and the stars blink. That was the setting when Rizzie told everyone, including Jumpy, that she had been diagnosed while still a teenager with schizophrenia. Her parents institutionalized her, but after nine months of Thorazine and other experiments performed at her expense, she'd had enough. She'd been on her own ever since. No one, including Jumpy, needed to know the details of what had brought her to the Poor Farm in Grand Lake Stream, because each one of them had their own details that perhaps didn't need to be known either. No one asked for more than what was offered—the Poor Farm's version of honor among thieves—and the result was a living arrangement that agreed with everyone.

Rizzie was going through one of her "good periods," but without medication, she was cautious about this, knowing from her own history that things could turn at any time. While speaking, she occasionally glanced up at Jumpy, watching closely for any sign of shock or dismay. She found neither. Jumpy had his own burden. He'd long been used to people keeping him at a polite distance due to his affliction. Rizzie hadn't done this, and now he knew why. It was a familiar Poor Farm story.

Falling in love was something neither of them had set out to do; it just seemed as if it were supposed to happen. Jumpy and Rizzie would become Jumpy and Rizzie, and to everyone else, it seemed like the natural order. Two seasons flew by, the second even more successful than the first. But that fall, after they'd found a pickup at an auto auction, Jumpy and Rizzie packed all their meager belongings into the takeout, hitched it to the truck, and left Grand Lake Stream. Some said Rizzie was beginning to feel a bad period coming over her and she didn't want to ruin things. Jumpy, by this time, was more than willing to navigate that, whatever it was and whatever it looked like, but what he wasn't willing to do was let her go. She'd embraced his erratic spells and taken them in stride, and now it was his turn. The rumor was that they were headed for Canada—even Guel said so.

People missed the takeout that next season. Tourists and sports asked about it so often at the Pine Tree Store that the store owners decided to open their own takeout to fill the gap. The Poor Farm eventually got so decrepit it seemed it was about to go down under the weight of the next big snowstorm or stiff wind, and it was demolished. The owner of the land sold it off, and a beautiful log home was built on the property by some folks with a long history in Grand Lake Stream. Some may have been glad to see the Poor Farm go. Others miss the days when Grand Lake Stream had a haven for folks from the margins, interesting people with their own unique stories and contributions. The Poor Farm kept to its own code of ethics, and the cast of characters who stayed there were often assets to the community. A town without esoteric personalities would have to be a dull place indeed.

4
Brody Talbot

Brody Talbot lived on land he inherited, land none of his ancestors had ever done anything with, and now that the last one of them was gone, it fell into his lap. The last one had been an aunt, his father's sister, who, on the very meager means of her disability check, had kept Brody in the old house, until finally it was she who was being taken care of by him, right up until her death. Brody had no education beyond the eighth grade, no vocational training, no skills beyond odd-jobbing and turning wrenches on motors. He found himself, at the age of thirty-eight, with the remains of a house that was falling in on itself. It was nearly impossible to heat, and worse, without his aunt's disability check, he had no means of feeding himself for the coming winter other than whatever he could catch or kill.

The postmistress in town had been friends with Brody's mother growing up, and she knew something about the family's dysfunctional history. During haying time that summer, she convinced a couple of the local farmers to hire Brody on. The days were long, the pay short, but it was something, and something was better than nothing. When that dried up, she sat down and put her mind to what Brody might be able to do. In order to tolerate his shortcomings, a person would have to have a good heart, she reasoned. The first person to pop into her mind was Guel Roberts at the Grand Lake Stream landfill. Why couldn't Brody be his assistant? Guel was getting on in years, and it might help to have a strong back handy for lifting and sorting heavier items. Because that's what Guel did—he sorted items according to what had value and what did not. Townspeople and summer people knew that whatever they dropped off at the dump did not necessarily meet its end there.

Guel was perhaps the wisest man that had ever presided over the landfill. He not only transformed the dump into a social center, he transformed trash into a lucrative second career. He'd worked in the woods all his life, following the industry from crosscut saw to chainsaw to mechanical harvesters and skidders. He'd had his share of injuries, of course, and now, in his sixties, he'd settled into a comparatively cushy job, greeting people and helping them unload. He accepted the postmistress' offer without hesitation.

For the first week, Brody did nothing but follow Guel around and watch him. This job looked to him like something he could do, even with his limited skill set. He was captivated. Like most people, he'd always thought that the dump was the dump, not the beginning of a new life for much of the booty brought there. He set his mind to learning from his new mentor, to knowing the difference between value and junk, and it was that summer that Brody discovered his calling.

Every Thursday, Guel made trips to Bangor with a truckload of what he called "merchandise." It was made up of items he had rescued from the great garbage maw where the town's trash was delivered weekly. By the time he made the trip, he'd already sorted the metals into separate categories, from valuable brass to lowly aluminum, and he'd saved everything, from trinkets to furniture that one of his collector contacts might rate as a worthy antique. Over the years, Guel brought this business to such a level of liquidity that the dump job served only as a supply chain for his markets. This was where he made his real money—as a middleman. Brody was beside himself. With his skimpy education and even skimpier qualifications, here was a slice of life he wouldn't have dared dream of, never mind pursue. He began to see his family's land out on the main drag in an entirely different light.

It took him a while to get permission to scavenge from several of the landfills in surrounding towns. He was careful not to trod on Guel's territory, and in return for the favor, Guel taught him as much as he could about junk. Brody had always had a speech impediment, which was seen in his youth as a kind of retardation. If you took that word in its literal sense—slowness—then they were probably right. The synapses in Brody's brain did perhaps take their time in sparking, but this was not necessarily a handicap in his new vocation and might just be an asset.

Soon, people began to notice space opening up behind Brody's shack on Route 1. He felled some trees and cleared away some brush. Then, month by month, passersby watched the gradual development of what appeared to be a fledgling junkyard. Though some locals didn't like it, it was also viewed with great interest for the new things that were showing up there. Apparently, once the word got out that you accepted junk, there was no end to what the world would enthusiastically deliver to you. In his second year of operation, a tattered, single-wide mobile home was towed to his property, and compared to what he had been living in, it was a vertical move for him. The trailer, with minimal interior work, became his home and office, and few could have missed the new bounce in Brody's step.

Inventory streamed into Brody's yard. Sometimes Guel would stop over to help him sort. Soon, he had to create paths through his property to give access to the many curious collectors who stopped in. Being on the tourist route did him no harm either, as out-of-state travelers sometimes stopped in just to see what the place was. They'd usually find something to buy, for no other reason than to strike a transaction with this quirky, colorful character. A shadow box. A galvanized washbasin. A pair of hay rake wheels for their removable dock at camp. Before long, Brody became a resource, albeit one that was never listed in any of the Maine tourism pamphlets.

There was more of a method to Brody's madness than there first appeared. I once showed up there after exhausting all my usual channels seeking the older style, numbered fry pans, in my case the#46, long-handled version for cooking fish during shore lunches. When I told Brody what I needed, he looked up at the ceiling in his office, scratched the stubble on his chin, and said, "C'mon." We walked about fifty feet, past several old wardrobes, a bathroom shower stall, a claw-foot bathtub, and five or six toilets, then took a left. This time, we walked past a couple of very rusted Glenwood wood cookstoves, some sections of Metalbestos chimney, two gas fireplace inserts, and finally some kitchen ranges, both in full and apartment sizes. That was where we took a right. Now we were really in the woods out behind Brody's trailer. We came to a pile of cookware, and beside it, under a plexiglass dome that must've once been someone's skylight, he even had a collection of flatware. As I stood there in amazement, Brody rummaged through the pile of pots and pans and came up with the exact thing I'd asked for. "Howzat?" he asked, looking up at me. My jaw dropped. When he'd looked up at the ceiling back in his trailer, he was locating this fry pan in his mind's eye. I'd seen as we walked how things were arranged vaguely according to what rooms in a house they belonged in. That was Brody's system, or structure, or methodology, though he would not have used any of those words.

Whether for simplicity's sake or because of an unusual taste in haberdashery, Brody developed a rather unorthodox "uniform." He wore pink rubber boots that came to his knees, purple sweatpants, and a blue, hooded sweatshirt jacket. Once he'd minted that look, he was never seen in anything else. He often had to repeat himself to customers who were not used to his speech impairment, but this only contributed to the mystique of the idiosyncratic character dressed in pink and purple who lived by the side of the road in a trailer surrounded by junk.

It was inevitable that a vehicle of some sort would eventually come his way. When a thirty-year-old flatbed pickup finally did, it cost Brody nothing but a double-axle trailer he'd taken in trade for something else. He now had the means to haul scrap metal for cash each time he'd built up enough to justify a trip. For the first time in his life, he had a real income. It might be an exaggeration to call it steady, because seven months of winter in Maine can make the most bustling business go crickets for a while. Even so, he could feed himself, heat the trailer, and still hunt and fish around his property, as he'd always loved doing.

Something, however, was brewing in the background on phone lines, over cribbage boards, and at the beano table on Friday nights. It certainly wasn't coming from the postmistress. She was proud of Brody, and told him so every chance she got, wishing that his mother was still alive to see how well he'd done. As for Guel, he'd mentored a protégé right into entrepreneurship, and Brody was still there for him whenever he needed him. It was a win-win all the way around. The trouble brewed quietly, like a forgotten batch of bad beer, fermenting in the dark and building up pressure.

In rural communities, resentment is always a byproduct of new upstarts, especially successful ones. Good fortune steals too much light, causing some in its shadow to feel diminished. Instead of admitting to this, the grousers will often devise a decoy pretext for helping the offending party down a few pegs while simultaneously casting themselves in a haloed light. In Brody's case, that pretext was the "eyesore factor." His junkyard was increasing and multiplying, to no one's benefit but his own, while advertising an Appalachian image for the visiting public—the community's bread and butter. In short, Brody's enterprise constituted an image problem for the town. This was the chatter, and chatter repeated often enough becomes conviction. The grumblers may not have made up a majority of townspeople, but they did comprise a voting bloc. Candidates for town office had better pay attention to this bloc, which, after all, was only concerned with the town's image and its future. They had nothing against Brody Talbot personally, of course.

The warrant, drafted and ready to be presented at town meeting in March, read, "That the property on the east side of

Route 1, three and one half miles from the Grand Lake Road turnoff, shall be declared a public nuisance due to unsightly debris deemed also to be environmentally unsound." It was language designed to make putting Brody out of business sound like a civic duty. The fact that the warrant, if enacted, would create a municipal dependent requiring public assistance in the place of someone gainfully employed and contributing to the tax base was a blind spot to the leaders of the charge. Brody would go back to being the old, inconsequential Brody, and his mess would be cleaned up.

It all came to pass. Brody had never been to a town meeting and didn't attend this one either. All through his childhood, he had been a laughingstock whenever he had to speak in front of the class, in Sunday school, or anywhere else. It was not something he needed to put himself through now. Guel kept out of local politics because he lived in a neighboring town.

There is no worse month to hold a town meeting than March. March is when all the bad batches of beer explode, when all the wintering chickens come home to roost—weight gain and high blood pressure; pent-up, unexpressed beefs; the psychic ill-effects of being a prisoner in your own home for seven or eight months; low light syndrome (otherwise known as Seasonal Affective Disorder)—all these things are the shrapnel inside the mail bomb that is opened at the town meeting each March. When this one was opened, people gave full-chested, red-faced, "impromptu" speeches that were, of course, well-rehearsed. "Our children shouldn't have to see something like that on the school bus," said one lady, aiming and pointing a finger with every syllable. "It sets a bad example." A man known for always getting to church early on Sunday mornings to get a front-row pew stood up and said, "We're known for our natural resources around here, and I don't think what Brody's got there is a natural resource." Heads bobbled up and down.

The prime movers, the authors of the cause, never spoke. Their work was done. They'd successfully incited a groundswell of public fervor at a time of year when fervor came easily, and now they watched with confidence as slips of paper were passed around for the vote. They already knew the outcome because of their phone work the night before. There were, it turned out, more dissenters than they'd projected, and they'd do their best in the days to come to find out who they were. But in the meantime, the warrant was passed, and funds were approved to cover the bulldozer and backhoe that would be dispatched to Brody's property in the spring.

Today, you'd never be able to guess the spot along Route 1 where Brody's junkyard was. It has grown in with weeds, pucker brush, and jack firs. If you tried to get information on Brody—his whereabouts or what became of him—you'd be hard-pressed to get a straight answer. At first there was a rumor that he'd moved several towns away and was trying to get the same thing going there, but that rumor was never proven. Another far more bleak rumor had him in a group home in Lewiston, taking supervised trips to the Y in a minivan. So far, that story hasn't been corroborated either. For the longest time, Guel expected Brody to just show up one day, perhaps hoping to go back to being his assistant. It hasn't happened.

The ones under the haloes still say that the eradication of an eyesore helped the town's image. Among themselves, at least, there is vigorous agreement on this point. It's best not to bring up the matter to the postmistress, however. She seethes behind the counter, weighing packages and dispensing stamps, whenever one of the culprits comes in. Now, she's glad Brody's mother isn't still alive to witness what's happened.

As for the rest of us, it isn't that our hearts are broken because a junkyard has disappeared. What we miss is that quirky, peculiarly endearing character, dressed in pink and purple, talking with too much tongue in his words, then heading out of town in his flatbed Ford, loaded to the hilt with chrome, brass, aluminum, caned chairs, hutches, bunk beds, and practically anything else under the sun. He took care of his business and didn't mind anybody else's, while separating his neighbors from their unwanted flotsam. And now, they're rid of him.

It seems that smaller communities, especially as they grow more gentrified, have less tolerance now than they once did for people they used to call "peculiar." These irregular sorts from society's fringe once had a place in rural towns. They were allowed for, and even if the children disobeyed their parents and made fun of them sometimes, they were included. Sometimes their labor could be put to good use at the sawmill, the town garage, or the landfill. We simply called them "characters." Sadly, there are fewer of them now. They seem to end up in group homes or shelters or roaming the streets of cities, their identities blurred with others doing the same thing.

I still think of Brody, leading me down those circuitous paths full of "merchandise" to my fry pan. I use that pan almost every day, and sometimes tell the story of Brody to sports from away while I'm frying their fish. At the end, they always ask, "Where is he now?" And my reply is always the same: "I wish I knew."

5

Vinnie Lobosco

When Vinnie Lobosco first came to town in the 1970s, Val Moore and Earl Bonness were still actively guiding sports every day on the waters in and around Grand Lake Stream. Since both guides often worked out of Weatherby's Lodge, where Vinnie booked his stay, it was inevitable that they'd be paired up.

Vinnie was a newbie, all right—Earl and Val picked that up right away. He'd done a little fishing with his father, growing up in Central New Jersey, but it was nothing like this. He'd even trailered up the boat and motor his dad had left him when he passed away. It was a fourteen-foot, open aluminum boat of the kind you could have bought from Sears Roebuck in his father's day. It was powered by a 1956 Johnson seven and a half-horse power outboard, the purple one with the white wings on the cowling.

"What'er you gonna do with that?" Earl asked him, seeing the boat parked outside Vinnie's cabin, where he met him in the morning.

"Oh, I don't know. I just thought I'd bring it along in case." The top of Vinnie's head came to about the fourth button on Earl's wool shirt. Vinnie was looking straight up when he spoke to him.

"In case? In case all the water drains outta these here lakes so they shrink down to the size of them puddles you got back in New Jersey?" Vinnie looked up at Earl, not knowing whether this was a joke or an insult, since Earl's expression was flat. The full measure of Earl's words hadn't hit its mark yet because

Vinnie hadn't seen the waters they'd be fishing. He'd gotten into town around midnight the night before, and the last three hours of the trip had just been getting from Bangor to Grand Lake Stream. He'd falsely assumed that, once he made it to Bangor from Warren, New Jersey, nothing in Maine could be too far away. Heading east, he'd almost hit a moose on Route 9, or The Airline, as it was called by locals. That had shaken him up so much he'd had to pull over and get his palpitations under control before starting out again.

Vinnie was following directions from a diary his dad had kept of the trip he'd taken up here after the war. He and a couple of army buddies had driven a Studebaker, pedal to the metal, swapping drivers so they could go the whole way without stopping, except for gas. They dropped the muffler and lost two hub caps on the Grand Lake Road, which was still dirt the whole ten miles from Route 1 into town. The trip was expensive and fraught with trouble, and the weather was terrible the whole time. Nevertheless, barely a spring passed while Vinnie was growing up that his father didn't recount every detail of that fishing trip once more. While telling these stories, Vinnie's dad sounded different than at any other time.

The handwriting in the diary was good, very good, just like most all of the penmanship Vinnie had seen among his parent's age group. The problem was that the leather-bound book was water-stained. Crucial turns on the route were blotted out, resulting in an unexpected visit by Vinnie to the Canadian border, where he asked for directions from a U.S. Border Patrol agent. It was close to eleven o'clock at night, and Vinnie had made a seventy-mile mistake. He'd gone thirty-five miles too far, and now he'd have to backtrack to make his turn on the Grand Lake Road.

The 1966 Volvo Vinnie was driving was cruising along with the boat trailer bouncing behind it when another moose appeared right next to his side view mirror, just as he made the turn off Route 1. The quick realization that the Grand Lake Road was now paved served to settle his nerves. When he reached Weatherby's, only one of the many cabins was lit up, and there was smoke coming out of a stovepipe on the roof. When Vinnie pushed the door open, he saw a note sticking out from under a small plate with several oatmeal raisin cookies on it. "Welcome, Vinnie!" was all it said.

That's as much as I know about how Vinnie Lobosco got here that first time, but he never missed a year after that until 2017, the year he died. He continued to be guided by Earl and Val through the '70s and '80s, but mostly it was Earl. By that time in the Old Trapper's guiding career, he was counting on his charms to take up for where his aging joints and diminishing agility left off. Luckily, he had an overabundance in that department. Ken and Charlene Sassi, owners of Weatherby's at the time, would have him show up after dinner in the sitting room, where the guests would assemble to be regaled by Earl's storytelling. In a region of the country where this art form seems almost to grow on trees, Earl Bonness was without equal. With his red bandana knotted around his neck and his trapper's hat in his hands, he would begin a story without any fanfare, small talk, or introduction. His audience would instantly be taken in. Without knowing what their interests were, what their backgrounds or economic status might be, he launched into the skill he was master of: telling tales from the woods and waters of Downeast Maine.

One story always stood out for Vinnie. Earl brought his listeners back to the days when the trains used to run all the way to Princeton, Maine, delivering sports from Philadelphia, New York, Boston, and beyond. In those days, folks mail-ordered merchandise, much the same as they do now through Amazon, and they'd often have their order in just a few days. Earl had decided to grow his income by guiding upland bird hunters in the fall. For that, he'd need a good bird dog. He found out he could mail-order one, and so, not long after that, he showed up at Kelly Depot to collect the German short-haired pointer sent to him all the way from Simsbury, Connecticut.

From the moment he hopped in the truck, the hound was all business. All the way home, he kept his nostrils pressed to the window Earl had left cracked open, his bobbed tail working like an outboard motor. Earl was heartened. This dog was going to teach him upland bird hunting, not the other way around.

The next morning, bright and early, Earl took him to Little River, just a couple miles out of town on a rough gravel road. Earl knew of some good bird covers out there, so he thought it the perfect venue for the dog to show his stuff. Earl got out of the truck with his sixteen-gauge Savage Fox side-by-side shotgun. He loaded both barrels with size seven and a half birdshot, slipped on his hunting vest with pockets weighted with shotgun shells, then opened the truck door. The dog leapt from the truck seat, landing some twenty feet away. He was headed straight for the river. Confused, Earl padded along after him. When he reached the river, he saw the pointer standing rigid, tail up, holding fast as if posing for a portrait. Earl walked over to him, but he never budged. When Earl looked down over the bank into the water, he saw a giant chain pickerel, feathering its fins in the lazy current. His gaze went from the fish to the dog, then back again.

"You're not a bird dog, are you?" he chided. "You're a fish dog!" The Weatherby's audience all chortled, and Earl smiled, happy to have his crowd right where he wanted them. As usual, they were so mesmerized by his timing, his delivery, his soft-spoken Downeast accent, that he could've led them any place he wanted. Finally, someone started clapping, and the others joined in. He'd masterfully fooled them into thinking he was finished.

When, to their delight, he resumed, he told them there were few fish his wife, Teckie, loved more than pickerel. Its sweet, white meat, as light and flaky as haddock, was a treat she'd never turn down. As the German shorthair looked on, Earl picked up a sturdy cedar bough nearby, then walked around to approach the pickerel from behind. The water there was scarcely a foot deep. The dog seemed more excited than ever when the belly-up fish was lifted by the gills out of the river. He jumped and barked all the way back to the truck. From the bench seat inside the pickup, he never took his eyes off the fish lying dead in the bed of the truck. For his part, Earl was much less excited. He'd paid good money for a purebred bird dog.

Once home, Earl kenneled the reluctant dog in the house and left him barking while he went back out and brought the fish into his shop. Everyone in town knew, even if Earl's audience didn't, that some of the best paddles and sharpest axes came from that shop. He sharpened the old-fashioned way, with a pedal-driven grindstone, and his paddles were more whittled than sculpted on a lathe. To a chorus of barking from the house, Earl took out his razor-sharp Barlow knife and slit open the belly of the nearly thirty-inch pickerel. With his hat in his hands and his head wagging side to side, Earl looked up at his audience.

"And lo and behold," he said, "a whole litter of baby woodcock fell out onto the bench." Every soul in the sitting room loved this grizzled, coarse old guide for teasing them, tricking them, and guiding them down a trail of endearing deception.

I started guiding Vinnie in the late '90s, after Earl and Val had retired. He still trailered the boat up, the same one with the same motor. I'm not sure it ever got wet in all the years I knew Vinnie. On our first day together, he told me that he'd gone out with Earl the previous year, Earl's last year of guiding. By that time, Earl had added to the tricks that helped keep his trade alive into his late eighties. Stepping ashore at lunchtime, he'd solemnly announce to Vinnie that he had to "go see a man about a horse." He'd then plod off into the woods, to the exact same spot every time, no matter which lunch ground it was. Once, when Vin's curiosity got the best of him, he told Earl after lunch that he had to go see the same man about the same horse. When he followed the well-worn trail to a well-watered tree, he noticed something odd. In the back of the tree was a knothole and, when Vinnie looked closely, he saw a bottle cap sticking out of it. It was a pint bottle of Black Velvet, half empty. Similarly, at the other lunch grounds they frequented, Vinnie could always find the special tree with the perfect knothole. He never spoke a word of his discovery to Earl, reasoning that, if a little nip at noon helped to keep the legendary Old Trapper going, he was all for it.

With a pair of thick-soled shoes on his feet, Vinnie may have stood five feet tall, but his head of thick, reddish-gray hair added another inch or two. He was not quite as wide as he was tall, but it was close. Between his weight and his wide wheelbase, he seemed more securely fastened to the earth than most. Vinnie made noise when he walked. That was because of the gear hanging from his belt. I don't think I could ever list those items without missing some, but there was a filet knife, a serrated scaling knife, a Leatherman-type tool, a hook extractor, nippers (essentially fingernail clippers), a Deliar scale, a small first aid kit with a belt loop on the back, an aluminum cup, flares, a compass, a tape measure, and a bottle of Old Woodsman insect repellant. Vinnie was prepared for anything that might happen to him on a fishing adventure, except for one thing. If he ever fell out of the canoe, he'd sink to the bottom like a tire iron.

I guided Vinnie right up to the year when he didn't show up. That was almost twenty years. You get to know someone when you fish with them for twenty years. It's a very different matter when you have two sports in your canoe. There may be gamesmanship, competition, old jealousies, or a history you don't know about. If they're related, there's a good chance there's a family secret you're never going to hear. If they're professional colleagues, one is likely ahead of the other in the pecking order, and you don't want to touch that with a ten-foot pole.

With the solo sport, it's entirely different. There's no third party to hear something they shouldn't, to interrupt, to contradict, or to question. The solo sport is free to let everything out of the bag and see how it looks in the daylight to his trusted friend and guide. He'll never be judged or criticized for his honesty.

Vinnie never married. By the time I met him, he had worked a whole career at Northrop Grumman in electronics. Ten years into our relationship, he told me about a "girlfriend" who worked at a convenience store near his house. For the next few years, I always asked how Diane was, and the answer was always, "Fine." Then one year I asked the same question, expecting the same trim answer, but Vinnie simply said, "She died." And that was that.

In his retirement, he converted a hobby into an income. He took in broken antique radios and fixed them. The image of him at a workbench surrounded by old Zeniths, Philcos, Emersons, and RCAs was an easy one for me to conjure. He also fixed crystal sets, old army radios, wooden console models, and even the earliest transistor radios. When the shop work was done, however, Vinnie's passion was ham, and I don't mean the cured kind. Before the Internet, before cell phones and social media, Vinnie was able to talk to people all over the world for free, in real time, any time he wanted. As a licensed ham operator, he was free to broadcast on amateur frequencies anywhere in the world and even into space. Years later, when Vinnie purchased a seasonal camp in Grand Lake Stream, he brought all of his ham equipment with him and began broadcasting from Big Lake.

There are few things a fishing guide values more than appreciation. In Vinnie's case, this was never verbal. Nor did it show up in the form of a tip. In twenty years, Vinnie never once tipped me, something that would have fellow guides shaking their heads. Tipping is the tool guides use to measure how well they've done for a client. Whether he didn't know this custom, or whether he had a personal law against it, I never brought up the subject with Vinnie. I didn't need to because I already knew how much he appreciated his days of guided fishing. It wasn't that it was evident when he was trolling for salmon; nor did he evince much excitement when he was battling a bass on his father's glass rod, strained to the breaking point. No. If you wanted to see the picture of contentment on Vinnie, you had to see him at lunch.

He knew all the routines. While I cleaned fish on my paddle blade in the stern, Vinnie, without speaking a word, would start unloading the items we knew needed to go ashore: picnic basket, canvas firewood bag, bow bag with all the cookware, cooler with cold drinks, our entrée, pickles, cheese, and condiments. Periodically, I'd glance up to see him smoothing the red and white checked tablecloth across the picnic table, or pulling the coffee pot out of the bow bag to fill it with lake water, or walking back to see if there were any trees with knotholes. Once he was satisfied that he'd done everything he could to assist and facilitate lunch, his favorite part of the day, he took his place at the picnic table, facing the water.

After I'd brought the fresh fish to the prep table, I'd unscrew the jar of Vlasik dill pickles and dump them into a stoneware pie plate. Beside it, I'd put a plate of sliced sharp cheddar cheese. While Vin went to work on those, I put the filets into the wet mix and let them sit while I cut up my potatoes and onions. When they were finished, I put the filets in the dry mix and shook them up, racked whatever meat I was cooking that day into a broiler basket, then started my fire. Unlike most sports, Vinnie wasn't watching me. In fact, unlike most sports, he never spoke a word while I worked. For many, this is the time when the floodgates open, when you realize you have a shadow behind you while you work, as if everything the fisherman forgot to say while fishing has suddenly come back to them. Not Vinnie. He continued to stare out on the water while slowly devouring both plates of hors d'oeuvres.

When the oil in the skillet is hot enough, the filets take no more than three minutes to cook. That's how Vin liked them: not sushi, and not too crisp. Just lightly browned on the outside, flaky and soft on the inside. Once they were in front of him, he'd resume his communion with the water, savoring every morsel of his fish. I'd time things so that Vinnie's jaws were always working, without any long waits in between courses. By now, my coffee water would be boiling, my ribs or pork loin or steaks would be leaning in front of the flames, and my potatoes and onions would be hissing and sizzling in the Greenfield frying pan with the two-and-a-half-foot handle. From time to time I'd glance over at Vin, looking like royalty.

"You good, Vin?"

"Oh yeah." Vin never took his heavy "tool belt" off at lunch. As a matter of fact, I don't think I ever saw him use one thing hanging from that belt. It's just that he wouldn't feel ready without it. When the main course was served, I knew that we wouldn't be launching into any big conversations. Vin was too busy. All the while, he'd keep staring out on the water. He appeared to be thinking about what he was eating, savoring it. Appreciating it. No one else did this quite so contemplatively or so solemnly. It lasted all the way through dessert and coffee too, and no food I brought ever went to waste.

After lunch, Vin always helped me clean up. He moved slowly in his later years, and even into his seventies, I never once saw him stumble or fall. As plugged into the earth as he was, with that low center of gravity, I think it would take a mighty stiff wind to budge him. We had the chance to test that on one trip.

Big Lake is just under thirteen thousand acres. Some say it has twenty-eight islands. Some say it has forty-two. This may depend on what you call an island. It may also depend on what time of year you're counting. Invisible shoals in June are islands in September. Not that you'd call them real estate, but there's enough ground there in some cases to pull up a canoe, pitch a tent, and start a fire. Some islands, on the other hand, are formidable landmasses, and Stone Island is one of those.

Vinnie and I weren't going to Stone Island on purpose. It was the ominous black sky behind us that was driving us there. A stony beach made for a rough landing, and the lunch ground there was well past its prime. Nevertheless, there was a good canopy of pine and hemlock, should we need shelter from the rain. Had it been just rain, I probably wouldn't be telling this story.

I've been hit by only two microbursts while guiding, and this was one of them. The problem is that you don't know ahead of time exactly what's coming. It looks like a fast-moving thunderstorm, and this one was still some distance away. But it was close to lunchtime anyway, and it so happened we were fishing near Stone Island, so we had a convenient place to stop.

"Vin, I'm going to get lunch going and see if we can beat that storm before we have to take cover," I said, pointing to the growing black cloud at the south end of the lake. That was fine with Vinnie, because anything was fine with Vinnie.

When I pulled up on the stony beach, I saw the walls of an ice shack that had blown in and beached there since the ice went out last spring. I knew exactly whose ice shack it had been. The previous February, we'd had one of those "blows" that needs a better name. There were sustained fifty-mile-per-hour winds, with gusts to seventy miles per hour. Fish Budgell's year-round residence was on the north shore of Big Lake. In the winter, he kept an ice shack within view of his house. When he had a spare moment, he'd either walk or snowmobile out to the shack, get the woodstove going, and try to jig up a salmon or maybe a mess of white perch. Ice fishing is always a very social activity, and so everyone in town knew that was Fish's shack.

The morning after that big blow, Fish got up, poured himself a cup of coffee, and walked over to the front window, looking out on the lake. Where there should have been an ice shack, there wasn't. He picked up his binoculars and glassed an object, only to see that it was the floor of his ice shack, with the woodstove sitting in its place where it always sat. The walls, the roof, the stovepipe, and everything else had blown away. Discouraged but concluding there wasn't much to be done about it, he set off for his morning paper at the Pine Tree Store. Making his entrance, he eyed Val Moore seated on the Liar's Bench off to the left as he came in. Fish knew that, in this town where everybody knew everybody, nothing moved quite so fast as gossip. He knew, and he was ready.

"Awful thing about yer shack, chum," Val chimed in. "That blow took everythin' 'cept the floor and woodstove, did she?" Val half grinned.

"Yessah," Fish fired back, straight-faced. "It's gonna be a bitch to heat that thing now."

This was the story I told Vinnie, in hopes of keeping his mind off what was rapidly approaching. There would certainly be a big blow involved, as well as gully-washing rain, no matter how brief. Once I had Vinnie situated with enough food to keep him busy, I dragged one of the ice shack's walls up to the tree line and positioned it, lean-to fashion, on the lee side of a giant pine. There were a few nails sticking out of the top edge of the wall, so I picked up a rock and banged them into the tree. Then I placed a few heavy, water-logged limbs along the bottom edge to secure it. Last, I retrieved a boat cushion from the canoe and set it under the lean-to in order to insulate Vinnie from lightning.

When the storm that turned out to be a microburst arrived, I had Vinnie sitting in his lean-to with a cup of coffee and a brownie, looking for all the world as if he were happy to be experiencing a strange new adventure. I ran back to pull the canoe as far up on land as I could and was still standing on the beach when the first wall of wind hit. It spun me around and sent me to my knees. I looked up in time to see it blow the remaining coals out of the fire pit and into the woods. The canoe immediately went sideways and began to rock violently. I made a futile attempt to secure it. When I looked up again, the woods were on fire twenty feet from where Vinnie was crouched. I grabbed the container that was nearest to me—a cooler in the canoe—swept it through the lake, and ran for the woods. It was the fastest I'd ever run, thanks to a tailwind that almost lifted me off the ground. The trip back was correspondingly slow. After five or six trips broadcasting coolers full of water over the flames, the rain came, mercifully—I wasn't gaining on the fire at all. I glanced over to Vinnie, with his rain slicker on, high and dry and still eating his brownie.

As fast as it came, the microburst departed, but not before twisting some of the tops of spruce and pine trees right off of their trunks. Stone Island wouldn't look the same for a while. Nor would the Grand Lake Road, as I found out later. The mini twister followed the road out of town, leaving limbs, treetops, and power lines down in its wake.

"You all right, Vin?"

"Oh yeah." But when he came out from under the lean-to, I could see that he was wet through. The rain had leaked down from the top edge of the ice shack wall onto Vinnie's neck faster than he could get his hood up. His shirt was soaked.

"Come see this," I said. Vin set his coffee cup on the table and followed me over to the canoe. The gas can, the boat seats, the cushions, and even the fire extinguisher were all afloat in ten inches of water. I'd never witnessed a faster accumulation of rain in as short a time. Rather than bail for the next twenty minutes, I decided to take the motor off and flip it. The sun came out, the sky cleared, and it was a brand-new day. Except that I could see Vinnie was not at all comfortable in his soaking wet shirt and pants. This gave me an idea.

One of our ongoing jokes was Vinnie's claim that there were only two moose in all these Maine woods –the two he'd seen on his first trip up here. At this point, he had thirty years of empirical evidence to draw from. He'd seen everything else in his woods travels with Earl and Val and me. Black bears, buck deer, foxes, otters, muskrats, beavers, bald eagles, even a fisher cat. If there were more moose in all this country than the two he'd seen, he would surely have seen one by now. And if there was one thing I knew about Vinnie Lobosco, it was that he was game for anything.

It was three o'clock when we reached the landing, three thirty when I dropped him off at his cabin at Weatherby's, and four o'clock when I picked him up again. I was stunned when he walked out of his cabin without his tool belt on. It occurred to me to make light of that fact, but I decided against it.

It was late August, and the days had shortened enough that, by five o'clock, the shadows were lengthening. By six, it was dark under the table. Ever since learning the word "crepuscular," I've loved trotting it out in front of sports when they have questions about deer or moose. It's true: these animals are abroad at twilight, so the most likely times to catch them on the move are dawn and dusk. And if I was going to win the wager I had with myself, the best place to go was out the Amazon Road. A logging road, it reaches from the Grand Lake Road all the way to Route 6 in Kossuth, Maine, a span of close to thirty miles through nothing but tracts of wilderness. There are deer and moose wintering habitats galore, and many a fall hunter has relied on GPS Waypoints and compass coordinates to navigate to their secret haunts.

All I'd said when I picked up Vin was, "Let's go for a ride." A purposeful mission to see a moose is a mission doomed from the start. I'd once guided a couple from Farmington, Connecticut, a dentist and his wife, who'd come to Grand Lake Stream not to fish but expressly "to see a moose." Sorry to hear those words spoken out loud, I set out with them in my canoe to the moosiest environs I know. I'd seen three and four at a time there, but always unintentionally. The difference on this day was that we were going there in order to see a moose. Lady Luck is affronted by that kind of impudence. Ever the flirt, she takes a bold advance poorly. I believe we saw every game animal that's listed in the Department of Inland Fisheries and Wildlife Manual, and a few that aren't. Every animal, that is, except a moose. That manual should include a footnote that says, "If you want to see a moose, don't go looking for one."

So I made light conversation all the way out the Amazon Road, pointing out landmarks I knew, woods roads that led to brook trout ponds, and others that led to secluded lakes I had yet to visit with Vinnie. The sun was long gone, and the last light was beginning to fade. We were twenty-five miles out the Amazon Road and I was running out of small talk when a dark shape showed itself on the side of the gravel road a hundred yards ahead of us. Instead of hitting the brakes, I let off the accelerator, since we were only traveling fifteen or twenty miles per hour. True to the breed, and just as I'd seen them do scores of times before, this cow moose stepped out into the road, turned away from us, and went into a trot, while we followed at a safe distance.

"A moose!" Vinnie effused, and effusiveness was a side of Vinnie I'd never witnessed in the fifteen years I'd guided him at that point.

"Naw. Can't be," I countered. "There *are* no moose in these woods." You never got a belly laugh out of Vinnie. What you got was a wide grin that stayed there all the way back to the cabin. It was almost as satisfying as watching him eat lunch.

In the later years, when Vinnie owned his own camp on Big Lake, he always brought the dog he'd rescued from a shelter back in Warren, New Jersey. Misty was her name, and she bit me the first time I met her. I could only think that, finally, Vinnie had a companion, after spending so many years alone. While fishing, he talked to her out loud, even though she was back at camp. When we fished Big Lake, we would go in and check on her at least once.

As age crept up, showing itself in some new way with each passing year, Vinnie wore it stoically. The wide stance was still good for side-to-side stability; it was the front-and-back "drifts" that sometimes got the best of him. Stepping out of the canoe onto the beach, his weight got over the gunwales before his back foot had a chance to catch up, and the next thing I knew, Vinnie was running down the beach, trying to stay upright.

Another anatomical change announced itself one year without warning. Loud reports from Vinnie's backside suddenly became commonplace, and Vinnie's response to this was to try to camouflage them. In this effort he used Misty as a prop. Vinnie would call out his beloved dog's name whenever he felt one of these microbursts impending, but his timing was always slightly off, with the effect that the blast and the bellow were syncopated instead of simultaneous. Since Vinnie kept a straight face, I had to, too. Sometimes, the work of a fishing guide is harder than you might think.

Love isn't a word that most men use to describe their feelings toward other men unless we're three sheets to the wind, and then, we love practically everybody. "I love ya, man, and the next round's on me." With men, it's time spent and moments shared that seem to accumulate into something we'll call affection, fellowship, camaraderie, anything but love. I knew both Earl Bonness and Val Moore quite well when I was a younger man, and I could never imagine them saying that they loved Vinnie Lobosco, nor would he have said it about them. But between us, we had close to fifty years of moments shared with Vinnie. We had the joy of watching someone who truly appreciated what we were doing. What's more, he never once complained on a slow fishing day. Even after he got his own place and his own boat, he still wanted to be guided, cooked for, perhaps pampered a little. A lifelong bachelor, it was an indulgence he allowed himself a few times every summer.

I wish I could say that I knew what happened to Vinnie. He had no family, other than a distant niece. The year after he failed to show up, a Christmas card to him was returned by a law firm, with a note saying simply that Mr. Lobosco was deceased. I called the firm, but they were not permitted to give me any information.

With that, I was free to imagine the ending for Vinnie that I would have wished for him. In that image, he's sitting at a picnic table, staring out on the water. Misty sits beside him, eyeing the lightly browned fish I've just set down (we took Misty with us on our last few trips together). Whatever it was out there where Vin was starring, he'd always looked at it longingly. So, in my image, when it came for him, he was more than willing.

6

Lights in the Night

Back in the 1990s, there was astronomical research that showed that Washington County, Maine, was second only to Area 51 in Nevada for UFO sightings in the U.S. The data came with an explanatory note that this conclusion did not necessarily mean that UFOs visit these two places more than anywhere else. Instead, it was the absence of ambient light in these locations that enabled humans to view the heavens more clearly.

Light created by cities is sometimes referred to as "sky glow," a more flattering term than its alternative name: "light pollution." On the other hand, the moon and the stars are "discreet light" sources. With the absence of heavily populated cities, mega-industrial complexes, and busy freeways, what we have in this remote part of Maine is a distinct lack of light pollution. Just like Area 51 in Nevada.

THE BURNING COUCH

Sonny had built his camp in a place on West Grand Lake where he'd been taking sports to lunch for years. The spot had many advantages: a natural granite ledge that formed a jetty against incoming breakers during big blows, a gravelly bottom of the kind favored by smallmouth bass for making their spawning nests, and proximity to some of the best togue and landlocked salmon fishing on the lake. Another aspect that Sonny liked every bit as much was that the footprint he chose for the camp faced north. This afforded unobstructed views of the night sky year-round.

I was lucky enough to pound a few nails in the construction of that camp, and even luckier to share a love of stargazing with Sonny. Many nights after a cookout, several games of horseshoes, and a singalong, we sat down by the water and watched. On more than one of those nights, we saw the effect of particles from the sun reaching gases in the earth's upper atmosphere to create the magical multicolored light show known as aurora borealis, or the northern lights. It's almost impossible to speak during one of these events, because any effort to form descriptive words is overpowered by an overwhelming awe.

And so, when Sonny came around to my camp one evening to tell me what he'd seen on the way along the dirt road, I listened intently. Coming from a friend and fellow stargazer, the story was true, I had no doubt. It was off in the direction of Dougherty Ridge, he said, a view afforded from one of the higher elevations on the road into his camp. It was a moonless night, and therefore devoid of discreet light. At first he thought he was seeing the lights of an oncoming plane. Then, when the light elongated and plunged downward, he was alarmed. Had the plane exploded? He hit the brakes and watched. The object seemed to get closer as it descended, all the while looking less and less like a plane, until Sonny rejected that idea altogether. The more he watched its slow-motion free fall, the more it looked like a burning couch! He watched it until it fell below the tree line, possibly right into the lake.

By this time in his life, Sonny had seen countless shooting stars, meteors, and slow-moving objects at extreme altitudes, presumably satellites orbiting the earth. But this—this wasn't that. The next day, we both checked the papers to see if any air disasters had been reported, and fortunately there were none. We also spoke to townspeople to see if anyone else had seen what he'd seen, and unfortunately, they had not. The easiest way to rule out incomprehensible experience is to doubt, then dismiss it as exaggeration or fantasy. Easy unless you happen to be the one who experienced it.

My turn came a few years later, and the first person I sought out afterward was Sonny. I knew he'd give my account all the credence it deserved, coming from a trusted fellow sky-watcher.

THE LIGHTS

The fall holiday now known as Indigenous Peoples' Day comes while the salmon season on Grand Lake Stream and West Grand Lake is still open. These days, one can see boats trolling for salmon in mid-October, even as temperatures are dipping below freezing. Back in the mid-1990s, salmon season was still open on Grand Lake Stream through October but closed on the lake. Boat traffic was nil. Camp owners had pulled their docks, boarded up their porches, drained the water line, and bid another season farewell. All except for two camp owners, but at the time, I thought my family and I were alone on the fifteen thousand-acre lake.

It's a time of year I love to be in camp. The woods roads, carpeted with yellow maple leaves, look like Dorothy's yellow brick road. Partridge roam the edges, pecking up gravel to help them digest the mast crop of berries bloating their gullets. Water levels have been drawn down, so it's a good time to work on a beach or breakwater.

My wife and I and our eleven-year-old son had blown out the kerosene lamps and candles and retired after several late rounds of UNO. It had been a misty evening, and now, on my final trip outdoors, I could see that a thick fog was settling over the lake. Had there been another light on in a camp across the lake, I wouldn't have been able to see it.

Of the many things that can be responsible for a rude awakening in the night, an elbow to the ribs isn't usually one of them. When I jackknifed up in bed and looked at Shelley, I thought it was morning. The whole camp was bathed in what I presumed was daylight. I glanced at the clock: 1:00 a.m. I looked back at Shelley in dismay, seeing her shadow on the wall behind her. When I followed her index finger to where she was pointing, I was forced to squint. A giant light, the candle power of which must have been equal to that of a Coast Guard cutter searchlight, was trained on our camp. My skin prickled, and beads of sweat formed on my brow. Without thinking, I slithered out of bed and onto the floor, then crawled toward the camp's front door. When I got there, I looked back at Shelley. I could see her just as well as if it had been three o'clock in the afternoon. The light never moved.

I cracked the front door just enough to put my ear up to the opening. Nothing. What on Earth, I wondered, could be out over the water, producing such a fierce light and not make a sound? There was no wind, and therefore there were no waves lapping on the beach. Everything remained frozen—Shelley and I blinded by a light so powerful that it prevented us from seeing anything around or behind it. Shelley had blankets pulled up under her chin. I was on the floor at the front door, wondering what to do. Then, as if making up my mind for me, the light changed its trajectory. It was suddenly trained on the shore to our left. At this, I opened the door more and stuck my head outside. Not a sound. But now that the light was not blinding me, I could see that, whatever this was, it seemed to be hovering over the water instead floating on it. There was no ripple, no wake as the light moved.

It moved not just forward but up and down. The shoreline was thick with eighty to one hundred-foot spruce, hemlock, and pine trees. The light, partly because of the fog and mist, had every characteristic of a searchlight, casting a bright beam onto shore. It began to travel along that shore, shining from treetops to trunks in rapid-fire motion, so rapid that it had taken in a quarter mile of shoreline in less than a minute. That shoreline comes out to a point in our section of the lake, and when the light reached that point, I stepped out on the deck of our camp. Still there was no sound in our cove, no disturbance. Out off the point, the light was suddenly joined by a second, seemingly identical light. Momentarily, the two of them shone down the cove toward our camp. Even through the fog and mist, the powerful beams lay on the lake surface like broad silver ribbons. Then, just as quickly, both disappeared around the point.

I remained on the deck. Out on the lake, the same rapid-fire surveillance or searching or probing continued, for I could see the reflections of these movements in the night sky despite the fog, so powerful were the lights. When it was finished, my anxiety subsided slightly, and I went inside to check on Shelley.

"What was that?" she implored.

"I have no idea," was all I could say. We had nothing to compare this experience to.

"If it wasn't in the water, it must have been flying," she theorized.

"But how could it be flying and not make any noise?" I countered. We agreed that the only time we felt threatened was when the light was close, shining blindingly into our camp. After that, we felt mostly shock and bewilderment. When we described everything to our son the next morning, he was angry with us for not waking him. This would have been the coolest story ever to tell his friends when we got home.

We found Sonny the next morning at his home in town. Shelley said, "You do the talking." He listened patiently to the whole story, then thought for a long moment, and said simply, "Ayuh." With that, I knew he believed me.

Before returning to camp, we needed to pick up some supplies from the Pine Tree Store in town. When we walked in, I saw, to my surprise, Dicky, Sonny's cousin from Massachusetts. It was then that he told me he was staying up at his camp on West Grand Lake.

"You were up there last night?" I hastened to ask.

"Yup."

"Did you happen to be up in the middle of the night?"

"Yup."

"Did you see anything odd?"

"Yup. And I sure as hell didn't know what it was."

"Lights?"

"Yes."

I felt a tremendous sense of relief. Someone else had seen something they couldn't explain—the same thing we'd seen.

So what were those lights? Early experimental drones being tested by the military in remote places where they'd be least likely to draw attention? In the mid-1990s, no one was talking about drones yet, but that technology was probably underway. It's the best guess I've come up with to explain it away, and for some people, that's what has to be done. But for others, it might make sense that, if there were explorations of our world going on, choosing those places with the least celestial luminance would allow this to go on (mostly) undetected.

THE BLACK MASS

Randy Julius was a distinguished president of the New England Outdoor Writers Association for many years. He was also a musician and an outdoorsman, and when we first met, it didn't take long to figure out we were brothers from different mothers. We had more in common, it turned out, than just our first names.

One of Randy's many outdoor pursuits was upland bird hunting. He had a camp near Passadumkeag, Maine, that he loved to visit in the fall. Passadumkeag is about halfway between Bangor and Lincoln, along Route 2, which parallels the Penobscot River.

From camp, Randy could investigate countless grouse covers with his beloved English pointers. October, therefore, was a month he looked forward to all year. As a writer, he could chronicle the cycles of game birds, waxing and waning as they do over long periods of time. Woodcock, too, flourished in these woods, especially following cold snaps. The migratory flyway of this coveted quarry begins in Nova Scotia and makes its way to Louisiana, interrupted by favorite stopovers like the ones near Randy's camp.

The heavens here are vivid on clear nights. It was on one such night that Randy had a life-changing experience, one that he was able to tell me about twenty-five years later in surprising detail.

Randy and a friend had been in camp for several days. The hunting had been productive. Birds were flushing close because it was early in the season: they hadn't been hunted much, and so they weren't flying at the least disturbance. That would certainly come later in the season, but for now, between twenty and forty wing shots per day were not uncommon. The only obstacle to great bagging averages was foliage. There were still lots of leaves that hadn't fallen, so when a bird went up in thick cover, your chances were about fifty-fifty.

All that hiking behind eager bird dogs all day produces big appetites and well-earned sleep. Randy and his friend had therefore turned in early. Rude awakenings apparently come in many different ways in these Maine woods. When Randy realized that something had woke him up and that he didn't know what it was, the first thing he did was glance at his watch. It was 1:00 a.m. Funny, I thought, hearing him tell this story. That was the same time of night that our rude awakening happened.

Something was different, or wrong, only it wasn't immediately clear what it was. Was it a sound or a vibration that had awakened him? Maybe it was both. Randy walked to one of the camp windows. It had been a clear, starlit night when he'd gone to bed. When he looked up, all he saw was blackness. Had a front moved in? There'd been none in the forecast, and like me, Randy was a weather buff. The sensation of a sound or vibration or some sort of odd "presence" persisted. Randy stepped outside. When he looked up this time, every follicle in his scalp tingled. There were indeed stars out. Just not right over the camp. What was above the camp was a gigantic elliptical shape—an object that blotted out the night sky above it. "A huge black mass," as Randy said. He described his initial physical reaction to seeing this as "cringing" or "shrinking" in fright. I could only imagine. I'd experienced a similar effect, but at least the phenomenon in my case was out over the lake, not hovering above my camp. When something ominous like a tornado is that close, you know what it is and what it can do. When something like this is that close, you know neither.

I knew Randy to be a serious person: reasonable, analytical, thoughtful. An extravagant imagination or an unusual predilection for sci-fi were not part of his profile. He woke up his friend, fearing that, if he did not, then it would be easy to dismiss what he was seeing, and he might even come to doubt it himself later on. Half asleep, his friend poked his head out. It was still there, only now its silhouette was more visible than before. Had it moved closer? To give scale to this object, Randy said that it was larger than the opening in the forest canopy where the camp sat. In other words, enormous. It seemed solid. They couldn't see through it. His friend was "freaked out," as Randy succinctly put it. So was he, but though he was practically paralyzed by fear at the giant foreign object hovering overhead, his curiosity forbade him to look away. He also knew that, whatever it was, though it was quiet, it must have some means of propulsion to have gotten where it was.

When it began to move, twenty minutes had passed. His friend had gone inside, but Randy called him back in a shouted whisper. "It's moving!" The two of them watched as the great, dark, amoeba-like mass moved slowly over the camp, revealing the shotgun blast of stars that it had been blocking from view. It seemed to take forever. It was still a toss-up whether it emitted a sound or a vibration, or both, but the sensation in Randy's chest was seismic.

When it was over, the two were disheveled, their nerves threadbare. Morning couldn't come fast enough. Neither of them was going to spend another night in camp after that. From then on, the story diverged. Randy could barely stop thinking about what he had seen. With that reasoning, analytical mind of his, he took to reading anything he could get his hands on about sightings, military operations, weather experiments—anything at all that might have been happening in the region to explain what he'd seen. And, like me, he came up empty-handed. That's a lonely feeling. At least he had one person who'd borne witness. That was consolation. But not for long.

Two people can see the same thing and walk away with completely different stories. Slowly, Randy realized that his friend was distancing himself. He didn't want to talk about the events of that October night; nor did he want to return to the camp for future outings. This isolated Randy even further. At the same time, he learned something vital. For some, finding themselves outside the comfortable boundaries of the normal and the expected necessitates denial; having the rug pulled out from under them this way is intolerable. A forced stare-down with the supernatural upsets tranquility, puts you on an uneven footing with a reality you thought you'd understood perfectly before.

In contrast, Randy embraced the experience. He knew what he had seen. Knew that it was real, even if it defied explanation. He came to accept that there are such things, and that to deny it doesn't make it any less true. He's met others, like me, who've had similar experiences. We haven't joined a club or created a society. We've had to assimilate something outside the realm of the known and move on, the richer for it. In the final analysis, our experiences were not harmful or threatening. Alarming? Yes. Disruptive? For sure. On the other hand, these two brothers from different mothers count themselves lucky for the privilege of having received a visitor peacefully, and having had our comfortable boundaries stretched.

The Stud Mill Triangle

The Stud Mill Road is an east-west dirt highway connecting Washington County to the Bangor region. Parts of it were built under Franklin Delano Roosevelt's Civilian Conservation Corps (CCC), a work relief program to aid the ailing economy and reduce the high unemployment rate among unmarried young men. Some of these men stood shoulder to shoulder with German soldiers from the prisoner-of-war camp located at the eastern end of the project.

As a vital artery for hauling wood chips, pulp, and tree-length logs from timbering operations to pulp and paper mills, the modern Stud Mill Road dates from the 1970s, when its construction cost timberland owners twenty thousand dollars per mile. With its many wilderness slag yards and tributaries, it quickly gained renown with UMaine college students and local high schoolers as a famous weekend destination.

You travel on the Stud Mill at your own risk, and at the pleasure of the logging contractors who have business there. Some may scream past you in a cloud of dust, trusting that you will have moved out of the way. Others may slow down, wave, and let you pass.

With the advent of the Stud Mill, a night out in the big city began to seem plausible for those who lived at its eastern end, provided you were willing to risk an hour and a half in the woods at night, out of range of any contact. Throughout the '80s and '90s, the then Performing Arts Center, (now the Collins Center for the Arts) on the main campus of the University of Maine in Orono, featured big acts with star power pull. When Suzy Bogguss was appearing there in the mid-'90s, my friend

Rocky, his wife Toni, and Shelley and I decided it was too good an opportunity to pass up.

We knew the hazards. Shale that is turned up after grading can easily puncture tires. If there has been a rain and the road is soft, washboarding occurs. A fifty-seven-mile ride over a washboarded surface can loosen the fillings in your teeth and blur your vision.

We were lucky. On concert night that June, the road was safely navigable at fifty miles per hour. Our spirits were high as we anticipated being part of an intimate audience in that setting, listening to a voice we all believed could heal the sick or tame the beast within. Suzy did not disappoint, singing her heart out to a full house and then hanging out afterward for a meet and greet. We came away with CDs, posters, and other paraphernalia to show everyone when we got back home.

By the time we reached the entrance to the Stud Mill in the rural town of Costigan, it was close to midnight. Stars reflected off the Penobscot River when we took our right turn off of Route 2 and passed the offices of what was then Champion Paper Company, later purchased by International Paper. When those lights were in our rear-view mirrors, I found a comfortable cruising speed around forty-five miles per hour, while Rocky hung back about a mile to avoid the dust I was kicking up. At forty-five miles per hour, I at least had a fighting chance to get out of the way of a moose who rightly believes he owns the road at night. The first test came about eight miles out. The bull moose that I caught up with turned his head sideways when my headlights hit him. Then he abruptly stopped. So did I. A lone bull moose in close proximity is never to be trusted. Things can swing either way with this moody animal, and this one weighed at least two-thirds as much as the Toyota I was driving. It was June, and his antlers were covered in soft velvet. As they continued to grow, they'd eventually slough off the velvet and calcify into weapons he could use against other bulls to mark his ground and show his dominance.

At a standoff, I slipped the shifter into reverse, just in case. Vehicles of all types all over Maine have been sent to junkyards after being charged by a bull moose. This one did look like he was considering it, but then must've decided we weren't worth the inconvenience. He started up again at a slow trot, then picked his preferred entrance into the thick spruce growth on the right and disappeared. As I was picking up speed, I saw Rocky's headlights clearing a rise in the distance behind us.

Back then, it was all wilderness. Within ten years' time, amid great controversy, a power line would be built alongside the Stud Mill, but such plans were not yet laid. A first quarter sliver of moon hung over the tree line in the east. Every constellation in the June sky was visible, including the little guy, Pleiades, out to play with his big friends, Leo, Ursa Minor, and Virgo. To be under a night sky so brilliant and so misleadingly close is to feel accompanied rather than alone.

The three red lights that showed up in the middle distance, at our ten o'clock, changed that feeling of accompaniment into mild curiosity. It was a good way away, so it could be anything, we reasoned. It was a weekend, after all, and sometimes the Air National Guard out of Bangor ran medivac exercises out here. Those lights could be from a chopper or some other aircraft, but at that distance, we couldn't tell.

Then, all of a sudden, we could. Why? Because, in the time it took for us to make our medivac guess, the object cut its distance from us to about four hundred yards. Shelley said later that I hit the brakes faster than I had for the bull moose—not only hit the brakes but killed the engine. It was as if the object had seen us and immediately zoomed in for a closer look. The Toyota 4Runner had manual, roll-down windows, and I slowly rolled the driver's side window down. For those lights to have raced that far in so short a time, they had to have a powerful engine. The Sikorsky Black Hawk helicopter was really coming

91

into its own by that time, though I had yet to see one. Many of the maneuvers I'd seen along the Stud Mill still involved leftover Hueys from the Vietnam era. Maybe this was my chance to get a close look at one of the newer models. If this was a copter, it had killed its engine too, for there was no sound in those woods other than crickets.

The lights were still in the direction of ten o'clock, but they seemed to be still. As we started up again, we realized we were getting closer. It turned out that there was a slag yard at the end of a short road perpendicular to the Stud Mill. A slag yard is area of an acre or so, left over from a logging operation. Skidders "twitch" whole trees out of the woods where they've been felled by mechanical harvesters to a "yard" that has been cleared for this purpose. A cherry picker piles them up for the logging trucks that will haul them to a mill. When the operation is finished, the yard is left with only debris: bark, limbs, tops, and sawdust.

When we reached the short road that led to the yard, we saw the object. Three shimmering red lights in the shape of a triangle floated at treetop height above the open slag yard. There was nothing between the lights, neither above nor below them, nor in the center of the triangle they formed. We could see stars right through it. Nor did anything seem to connect the lights. "Let's go!" Shelley said in a loud whisper. The sight was unnerving, making no noise whatever. There were no cell towers at the time (and there still aren't out there!), but this object wasn't attached to the ground the way a tower would be. Once again, it was the absence of any sound that was the most unsettling thing.

Neither of us had spoken for several miles when I remembered Rocky. I immediately pulled over and waited. It was long enough before I saw his lights that I assumed he must've stopped too. When he pulled up behind us, I was standing beside my truck. Rocky got out and walked toward me.

"Did you see those lights?" I asked.

"Which ones?" he replied. It turned out that they had seen not only the ones we'd spotted, but also a similar set earlier that we had missed.

"Any ideas?" I asked.

"Not a one," he replied.

What was once a foreign concept to us is now familiar. Even so, unexplained phenomena that slip suddenly into our immediate presence still produce fear. But so far, none of our encounters have resulted in anything but fear. And awe. We are never dismissive when someone else has the courage to tell us what they've seen, no matter how outlandish it may seem. They get no derision or disparagement from us. We always lend an ear.

7

Valkyrie

The day and the destination were all planned from the time the job was booked. The dad wanted to take his son on a tour of West Grand Lake. He'd been brought here by his own father when he was eleven, and that was the age his son had just reached this summer. The dad had never gotten over the impression the trip made on him all those years ago, and now he wanted to relive it with his own son. I was the guide he hired.

Heading uplake from the boat launch on the west side of the dam, I brought my canoe in close to a series of rock piles encased in logs sticking up out of the water. They are cribworks. Their function up until seventy-five years ago, was to anchor large booms of logs before they were let, piecemeal, down Grand Lake Stream in the spring. That was when there would be sufficient "heads" of water to push the logs downstream, and eventually to their destination—a mill. In those days, there were fourteen-year-olds who knew how to use dynamite to disrupt logjams in the river. With father and son sitting in front of me, I threw that in just to pique the boy's interest. Then I told him that, if he saw these cribworks before they were filled with rocks, he'd say they looked like Lincoln logs, spiked together up to a height of ten or twelve feet. Once they were filled with stone, they weren't going anywhere, and they haven't for a hundred years.

The boy never even looked over the side of the canoe to see what I was talking about. His face was six inches from a cell phone screen, while his father took it all in, craning his neck to see all the way to the bottom. We picked up speed after the second cribworks, and only slowed down a little when we came to Munson Island about ten minutes later. Maybe an island, completely self-powered, where visitors came on floatplanes, would interest a boy. I talked about the year-round caretaker, a friend of mine, and his wife, who looked after the place all year, not just in the summer. In March, they cut giant squares of ice out of the lake and buried them in sawdust in an icehouse on the island. All summer long, the guests had ice-cold drinks as well as refrigeration because of this practice, which had been going on for generations. They used to use special long-handled ice saws with a special type of teeth that was best for cutting ice. Nowadays, they used chain saws, but they still fetched the chunks out of the lake with big ice tongs. They were then put on toboggans or tote sleds or skids, depending on the era, and towed right up onshore to the ice house. I was making the story as graphic as I could in order to capture the interest of the boy, but he never looked up. His dad was enthralled.

"And they still do that to this day?"

"Absolutely," I replied. "In fact, I saw pictures of the operation online this past spring. My friend, the caretaker, got the whole family involved."

"Unbelievable," he said, shaking his head. I looked at the boy. Nothing. I scratched my chin. Maybe a big fish story would do it. A few minutes later, we passed Crescent Moon, a rock formation, which, in August, is very visible in the crystal-clear waters of West Grand Lake. A guide friend of mine had taken his sports trolling right next to Crescent Moon the previous year in late May. The water was still ice-cold, and my friend knew that togue (lake trout) were apt to be hanging around shoals like this one, looking for smelts. When the fly rod one of the sports was using was yanked out of his hand, the guide's reflexes were razor-sharp. He caught the rod, thinking the fly had fetched up on one of the sharp granite boulders that make up Crescent Moon. Wrong! There was life on that line! He handed it back to the sport, shouting, "Reel!" Though it was his biggest fish ever, the sport did everything right for the next ten minutes, raising his rod tip as the fish finally came within pole netting distance of the canoe. First swipe and the guide had him! The togue was so large he took up the whole width of the canoe's floor at the man's feet.

I waited. This was where, as a boy myself, I would demand to know the weight, the length, every detail. I waited some more. Not a peep, until the dad asked, "So how much did it weigh?" I looked at his son. His thumbs were moving a mile a minute. A game of some kind had his full attention. "Just over ten pounds," I answered.

We traveled another twenty minutes before I slowed down long enough to say to the dad, "Maybe you remember Caribou Rock?" as I pointed to it over his right shoulder. He turned, but the boy did not. "Yes! Yes! I sure do! Magnificent!" Less than a mile away, I slowed again near Columbus Island. I wanted to see whether Delilah, my pet name for the eagle that had birthed twins there in June, might be perched on one of her favorite tree limbs. I killed the motor and took up my paddle. The father picked up a spinning rod and made a cast. When I saw the swirl and then the explosive splash, I yelled, "Fish On!" louder than necessary. The boy, evidently at a key moment in the game on his phone, kept busy. Frustrated, I netted the hefty smallmouth bass and purposely dropped him at the boy's feet. He looked up from his phone only momentarily.

"My God! I think my dad took me here," the dad blurted out. "We picked blueberries and ate them—the best I ever had!" I paddled in closer until he could reach them. "Look, Jay! Wild blueberries! Taste these..." The boy put his arm out toward his father, cupped his hand, and brought berries back to his mouth, never looking up.

When I'd given up on Delilah and was preparing to start the motor, we all heard an enormous whoosh of wings, but only two of us looked up. She had waited until we were right under her, hidden by thick spruce boughs, then took off so that we could see the full span of her wings and her giant talons before she folded them in for flight. I imagined Delilah laughing at having gotten the drop on me so well this time. The dad's mouth was agape.

When we entered The Narrows at the head of the lake, there was a calf moose standing on the promontory that juts out on the right side. She probably weighed two hundred pounds. When I pointed, the father turned, but of course his son never saw me pointing. I touched his shin with the toe of my boot. When he looked up, annoyed, I pointed again. He did look, but not for very long.

Up ahead was a story newcomers love to hear. I wondered if the dad had heard about Coffin Point. I reminded him of the tannery in town early in the last century and how they used hemlock for tanning liquor. The bark was harvested all around the lakes from camps where men lived and worked, getting their supplies only when the steamers towing barges came to pick up the bark. Sometimes men died there: injuries sustained on the job, illnesses, infections, or accidents were the most common causes. The body of the deceased would be placed in a makeshift coffin, perhaps not the permanent one for burial, but enough to get it to town and then to an undertaker. I closely watched the boy in front of me during this part. What eleven-year-old boy wouldn't perk up for a story with a dead body in it?

His father, who'd never heard it, was waiting for me to go on. West Grand Lake, as he knew, was famous for sudden changes of weather. Storms came up fast enough to put people in trouble before they had time to dodge it. And one did. The steamer was able to negotiate the sudden sea, but the barge, top-heavy with hemlock, capsized. The body was lost and all we have today to commemorate the event is the name of the place where it happened. Coffin Point has appeared on maps for generations. The watery tomb of the unknown hemlock harvester lies somewhere off that point, "right about here," I said as I passed over the spot. I was sure I'd see some reaction from the busy boy in front of me, but he must have been at a critical point in his game. His thumbs were moving, his brow was furrowed, his eyes still six inches from the screen. "My, my, my," his father said, appearing lost in thought. Then he told me something he did remember from his trip here long ago. "It was like something out of *Twenty Thousand Leagues Under the Sea*," he said, referring to the Jules Verne classic made into a Disney movie when he was a kid. "Got it!" I replied. I throttled up and headed south, down through the Thoroughfare into Pocumcus Lake, and then west through Pocumcus Narrows. It was one of those perfect August days. You could see but not feel a hint of autumn as the late summer sky reflected a deep blue on the lake. The edges of some of the maple leaves were tipping red, and these reflected onto the water as I proceeded at steerage speed through the passage. When we rounded the final turn at the end, I pointed over the man's left shoulder. We could now see Dobsis Dam and the fish ladder next to it. Water from Sysladobsis Lake cascaded over the dam and down the fish ladder into the stream below. "Look, Jay!" the man said to his son. He was pointing toward a huge object that appeared to be half-sunk. The boy didn't respond, but I swung the canoe in close, putting the derelict alongside the canoe. It was a mass of rusted steel. You could see from the part that was showing where huge sections had been riveted together. The object was rounded in shape, almost reminiscent of a miniature submarine. "That's it! My God, just the way I remembered it," Jay's father exclaimed. It was true. I'd been seeing it for forty years, and the only recognizable change was how much of it was sticking up out of the water when lake levels rose or fell. It weighed so much; it wasn't going anywhere. I told him I believed it to be the boiler from one of the steam vessels that were used to haul sports, canoes, and supplies up to Sysladobsis Lake between the First and Second World Wars. I took a few back strokes with my paddle until we drifted around to the opening of the canal. This was where boats or barges could be pulled from Pocumcus Lake into Sysladobsis Lake, with the help of pulleys, rope, chains, and horses—very nearly a miniature version of the Panama Canal. I watched it all settle over the man's face, as though he had time-traveled back and was watching it happen. "Marvelous!" he effused. "My God, the ingenuity!"

I told him there are moving pictures of this entire region, preserved by an institute in Maine that specializes in historic film. These movies were probably taken on a Kodak Brownie, one of the first movie cameras available to the public, beginning around 1910. I'd seen these films, showing portages, hunting trips, big game hunts, the resulting trophies, and the like.

We took our lunch near Dobsis Dam, beneath a stand of tall pines between the canal and the stream. I thought for sure the boy would want to set out to explore the area. Sometimes, especially at this time of year, you might see salmon pooling above the dam, preparing to drop down into the stream for spawning in the fall. I mentioned this as the boy found a round rock to sit on. I went on to describe the "redds" that the salmon would build on the stream bed: mounds of gravel with an open crater where the female would deposit her eggs. Then, with a lot of vigorous tail-fanning, the crater was filled back in, protecting the eggs from harm. Months later, tiny alevins would squirm their way out of the gravel to begin the hard life of an infant salmon. I had an audience of one. During cleanup, the father pitched in, helping me make short work of it, but the boy's head never came up. I had two more rounds of ammunition, and I meant to use them on our way back. If they didn't work, nothing would.

In half an hour, we were almost to Coffin Point when I slowed the motor and turned the canoe so that we could all look northward. "Bear Island," I said, framing the long expanse of its landmass with both hands. "Bear Island," the dad repeated. "There's gotta be a story there." There was. Blood, gore, a bear, death: all of the big guns for an eleven-year-old boy.

Alonzo Bacon, brother of Herbert "Beaver" Bacon, inventor of the Grand Laker Canoe, was here on a hunting trip in the very early 1900s. In all likelihood, there was just one reason a party of hunters would land on an island of this size in the fall of the year, though that reason might be frowned upon in our time. Deer end up on such islands, sometimes after being chased into the lake from the mainland by a predator. They actually do quite well on these large islands, most of which have bountiful mast crops of nuts and berries from beech trees, as well as raspberry, blueberry, and blackberry bushes. Also, they are probably safer here from predators, except for one–man. Driving deer anywhere, much less on an island, is illegal in the state of Maine today, but it was probably more common then. Rather than impose a moral judgment from our time onto Herbert and Alonzo, I prefer to say that times were lean and meat scarce, and who is prepared to second-guess what a man might do to provide for his family? In any case, the color of this hunt was brown, not black. Even so, in hard times, a hunter was not going to pass up a shot at a bear.

Safety was not the concern then that it is today. Blaze orange was a thing of the distant future. Hunters wore whatever was warm but light enough to walk in without overheating. Usually that was wool. Was Alonzo wearing black? Had he been stalking, perhaps low to the ground, inspecting a track, or stepping lithely over a blowdown when one of the hunters in the party saw the dark shape? We'll never know. All we do know is that the hunter fired. The round took Alonzo in the thigh, and he surely let out a scream. Imagine the horror the shooter must have felt upon hearing it. The party rushed to him, got a tourniquet around the leg above the wound, then carried him to the canoes. One can only imagine the dread and haste of the moment, the life-or-death paddle strokes the whole twelve miles downlake in the days before outboard motors. Except that, after just a few miles, it wasn't necessary to rush. Somewhere between The Narrows and the dam at Grand Lake Stream, Alonzo expired. I see heads lowered and shoulders rounded in those canoes. I see people meeting them at the landing, wondering why they were back so early. People waiting to see the horns of a big buck sticking up above the gunwales. Blood had surely pooled on the floor between the ash ribs, swashing back and forth with every stroke. Alonzo lay in the arms of the man who had mistaken him for a bear. Presumably his was the last voice Alonzo heard, beseeching him to hang on.

"And that's why it's called Bear Island," the father said when we were halfway down the lake, going only at trolling speed so he could hear me. "Yes," I answered, eyes on the boy, who suddenly piped up, startling both his dad and me: "Hey! There's no signal!"

I asked him what game he was playing on his phone.

"Valkyrie," he said, annoyed.

I picked up speed until we'd just passed Brown's Rock, on the shoreline to our right. You could barely make out the "Brown" that had been etched into the broad granite face sometime after Eddie Brown caught his twenty-eight-pound togue here. He'd been fishing through the ice when he pulled up the monster. We weren't very far from shore when my bow passenger asked, "How deep is it here?" I told him about ninety feet, which impressed him. I picked up speed for another several hundred yards, then killed the motor at Steamboat Cove.

"Back in tannery times, those steamers had a shelf life," I began, "and when their time came, they brought them here and burned them to the waterline." I looked at the eleven-year-old for some sign that he'd heard me. A boat being purposely set ablaze on the lake might have moved me at that age, were I to have heard about such a thing. "By the time they were burned, they were basically useless. But some parts of value would still be aboard when they sank to the bottom. Years ago, a friend of mine went diving here and came up with a propeller from one of the steamers. He held onto until his death in 1994 but left it to me in his will because I'd always admired it so." Cell signal must have returned, because my final piece of ammunition had been lost on its target. His dad, however, took great interest. "I bet it was brass," he chanced. "Right! And worth a pretty penny," I added.

I could tell the dad hated to see the day end as he helped me load the canoe onto the trailer. He even reeled it up on the winch while I guided it on the rollers—something very few sports take part in. I looked around, but his son had already walked up to their car. I made every effort not to bring up what I'd witnessed that day, even though it weighed on me heavily. In fact, that effort may have shown on my face, because, as we finished tying down the canoe, the man began,

"I want to thank you for today. My son's not very social. I guess you figured that out. He's a straight-A student in school, in classes for gifted kids. He has trouble connecting with others. It took some convincing to get him to come up here with me. My hope is that something from this day will seep through. And it just might, even if it takes months or years. That's the way it goes with him."

We settled up, and I shook his hand, then took a burlap package out of my canoe bag and handed it to him. He opened the burlap to find a hookaroon (the whittled branch from a sapling we use to manage hot handles and bales on the lunch ground) and a fistful of cedar kindling sticks wrapped in birch bark. "Give this to Jay for me, please. Tell him he can always start a fire with this if he ever finds himself in a survival situation."

Jay had been in a survival situation all day. A virtual one. Something in him sought that out—a sensorial world of sound and fast action that muted the real world around him. The game, ironically enough, is named after Valkyrie, the Norse goddess who decides who lives and who dies in battle. How much of the day, I wondered, had "seeped through," as Jay's father hoped it might? I don't know. All I do know is that, the week before Christmas, I got a card from his father. Enclosed was a note, on which he wrote, "Jay keeps that burlap hookie-something you gave him on his dresser. My wife has moved it several times, but he always puts it back there."

That was all I needed to hear.

8
Dukes of Haphazard

Around the start of the new millennium, sports and other visitors traveling down Water Street toward Big Lake would notice a property along the way that left them searching for words. What could explain this incongruous ninety feet of frontage in the otherwise charming, quaint community? Passing slowly by, mouths agape, they saw furniture, blankets, mattresses torn open, a crushed canoe, a mangled swing set, a vehicle up on blocks, exercise machines, a sink or two, as well as a couple of toilets, lumber, plastic, and a few unidentifiable objects. Some even observed that this was an odd location for the town landfill.

A garage attached to the house where much of this refuse might have been hidden was itself filled with even more. Moreover, the garage door was perpetually open, its contents spilling out into the driveway. "Does someone live there?" an astonished sport would invariably ask. "Yes," came the standard answer. "Our mayor."

It was, of course, a ruse. Grand Lake Stream has no mayor, nor a mayoral form of government. It has instead three town assessors, each of whom serves a term of one year, after which they can run for reelection as many times as they like. Sometimes the term "selectmen" is used interchangeably for "assessors," but these days, that term has fallen from grace as many, if not most, of these officials are women. And so the gender-neutral term "assessors" turns out to be the perfect fit.

While there are three assessors, there tends to be a built-in hierarchy, if for no other reason than that they run for first, second, or third assessor, and so a descending degree of importance is attached to the numbers. Whoever wins first assessor carries a little more gravitas than the second, and the second in turn carries more than the third. Sometimes these titles are affectionately abbreviated to "first ass," "second ass," and "third ass," which serves a dual purpose. One use is that it has a leavening effect on the governance of a town of scarcely seventy-five people. We are, after all, not dealing with a high crime rate (or any crime rate at all). There is no police force, no gang, mob, or even traffic. For the most part, the business at hand is a streetlight that was shot out during hunting season, or a dispute between parties who claim to have dibs on the same cemetery plot.

The second purpose served is as a reminder to our elected officials not to take themselves too seriously, since no one else does. And still, as you might already have guessed, the exception to this rule rears its head every once in a while, with a first ass who struts about officiously, as if the stability of the free world hinges on the governance of Grand Lake Stream.

Fans of the 1980s TV series *Dukes of Hazard* will remember the town's mayor, whose real name was Jefferson Davis, a wink to the Old South. But between his gluttony, his bottomless appetite for schemes that might allow him to reap a monetary reward, and the way he threw his more-than-ample weight around, he earned a nickname that stuck. The resemblance to a bumptious Grand Lake Stream town boss was just too great, and this particular first ass came to be known, affectionately or otherwise, as Boss Hogg.

His election to that position was a subject of enough controversy to fuel Liar's Bench discussions in the Pine Tree Store for several weeks. It was true that Boss Hogg had worked the phones hard in the days leading up to the election. But why, the day after the election, did fourteen of the headstones in the town cemetery have stickers on them that read "I Voted Today"?

This question was asked repeatedly on the Liar's Bench, where no stone is left unturned.

Apparently being both a bachelor and the town's biggest cheese wasn't the look Boss Hogg was going for, so he began to run classified ads looking for love. Since there was no newspaper that offered such a thing in or near Grand Lake Stream, these ads ran in some of Maine's larger cities. Confirming that the world is full of the lovesick and the forlorn, there was an immediate response. Word reached the Bench that there would be a rendezvous in Bangor, a recon mission for both parties. Or so they thought. To the amazement of all, Boss Hogg returned with his prize the same day, happy that, as a precaution, he had made a skunk path through his front yard to the door before leaving.

The Liar's Bench erupted. How had Boss Hogg managed to sell this much-younger gal on the life she was now stepping into, and dragging a daughter along with her to boot? Had he brought rose-colored glasses with him to Bangor to present her with? Had he glossed up his story so that the poor woman envisioned herself moving into a mayoral mansion? Did she think she was to be a public figure, hosting and entertaining dignitaries? One could only guess at the reaction of Grand Lake Stream's new first lady when she made her way up the skunk path to the hovel that was to be her new home.

Nonetheless, they concluded, it must have been love, for the next buzz on the Bench was that a spring wedding was planned for the end of the month. It was not to be a large affair. No dinner or ball. Just a small ceremony with a few family members and friends.

The occasion presented a problem. Boss Hogg had not attempted to don a suit for decades. He therefore excavated his most recent one and had it let out to its fullest capacity. Even then, the fit, to put it politely, was extremely restrictive. Their options were either to keep the ceremony short, or to have the town EMTs standing by with oxygen and defibrillator. They chose the former.

Boss's mail-order bride, according to the account of one guest, made a splash in what was revealed to be her red prom dress from twenty years earlier. It wasn't quite the strangulating fit of her groom's ensemble, but this observer said it created an impression vaguely similar to Little Bo Peep. Apparently one almost had to squint to see the bride's very slight young daughter hiding behind the folds of her mother's red regalia, looking for all the world like a wraith who had just stepped out of the forest, looking for food.

Townsfolk did the best they could to set out the welcome mat for the newcomers, but these efforts were frustrated by an initial reclusiveness on the part of both mother and daughter. For weeks on end there would be no sightings of them. The Liar's Bench was starving for news. Speculation that they were hard at work renovating Boss Hogg's hovel got a little bit of traction, but then fizzled when the third ass had to drop off a document and saw the same dingy bachelor digs as had existed before the nuptials. So what were they doing in there? Witchery? The dark arts? Winters are long, and the Liar's Bench is nothing if not a seedbed for active imaginations.

As summer came around, mother and daughter emerged from the confines of Boss Hogg's hovel, but never ventured far. The post office was less than a five-minute walk, the store another two. She returned greetings with a cautious smile at first, as though consorting with strangers was an unfamiliar business for her. This softened somewhat over time, but she and her daughter never lingered long in any one place. In fact, when you did see them, they were always on their way to or fro. The one thing everybody noticed, though, was the large black pocketbook slung over the mom's shoulder. On her other side, the home-schooled daughter walked so close as to look attached to her mother at the hip. She was never seen alone, and when she was seen, it was always in an appendage-like posture, nearly hidden under her mother's shoulder.

These oddities, in fairness, may have been nothing more than idiosyncrasies, of which Grand Lake Stream has more than its fair share. But to attribute such fertile fodder to mere quirks would make life on the Liar's Bench much too drab. The Bench was where theories and hypotheses were formulated. Any news could be worked into whatever elaborate plot that caffeine-fueled assemblage was currently weaving.

By the Fourth of July, they were all enlivened by a whole new turn in the mystery. Boss Hogg had apparently decided that one of his caretaking jobs was too taxing for him to handle alone. It involved keeping the grass cut on one of the largest lawns in Grand Lake Stream. The Bench soon heard of the sighting of Boss's bride behind a push mower, with her black pocketbook swinging from her shoulder. Her daughter tried with difficulty to walk beside her as she mowed. The woman had evidently never mowed a lawn. From one spot, she pushed the mower out and back, then turned slightly and repeated this until she had mowed a complete circle around herself and her daughter. Then she calmly stepped outside that circle, took a few steps, and started another. The whiskered geezer telling the tale to his audience on the Bench stood up to mime the maneuver, until spasms of laughter and hacking drowned him out.

Then, as if the ongoing saga of Little Bo Peep (a handle that unfortunately clung to the First Lady after the wedding) needed an injection of even more intrigue, it came to light that, in that black bag slung over her shoulder, there was a pistol. One day, while she was walking home with her daughter after mowing her husband's client's lawn, a pickup truck full of boys who were obviously "on something" pulled up beside her. The girls kept walking, eyes forward, but the vehicle crept along beside them. Out of the windows came catcalls and anatomical references, which prompted Bo Peep to reach into her purse and pull out the piece. "Whoah!" the yahoos said, holding up their hands. The woman waved them on their merry way with the barrel of a .38 caliber handgun.

After that, a whole new aura surrounded Little Bo Peep. Speculation had the Bench in a dither. Was she an ex-con? Was she carrying due to a perpetual paranoia related to her life before Boss Hogg? Just knowing there was a gun in that purse had the effect of drawing an imaginary "safe zone" around her wherever she went. Which was nowhere, except post office, store, and inside the crop circles she created on that massive lawn.

Maybe, they speculated, she was indeed on the run from something previous, something from which Boss Hogg provided the perfect escape . But that past, we mustn't forget, was a complete fabrication by a group of geezers starved for stimulation. Even so, if they hoped that the plot would thicken, they got their wish, and then some.

Boss Hogg's tenure as first ass had already exceeded the life expectancy of most of his predecessors. He had, it seemed, a good thing going. There was an income associated with the job, but it was inconsequential compared to what might be possible if you played your cards right. Just like in Washington, one might say. The potential for upgrading your personal portfolio lies in the influence you can wield. Who will get the contract to plow or pave the roads? Who will renovate the town hall, or build an addition onto the Historical Society building? How will federal grant money received for infrastructure be used, and how will those expenditures be prioritized? These areas, if you're in a position to do it and are so disposed, are where you can turn lead into gold.

The principal pastime of the Bench was to notice things. And notice they did. A brand-new truck with options replaced the beater Hogg had been driving since well before his rise to power. Then a new car showed up in the driveway of the mayoral mansion, which, it should be noted, hadn't changed in appearance since our story began. In fact, out-of-towners had begun to photograph it. Was it art? Was it a statement of some kind? A message? A chunk of Appalachia perhaps, pickup up and plunked down in this tiny northern town?

When news reached the Bench that a new tractor with an assortment of attachments had been added to the Boss Hogg fleet, their chin-wagging went into overdrive. There's nothing like a local suddenly moving into a higher socio-economic category to incite a quiet uproar. And that's what happened. Boss Hogg, they whispered, must have been moving pieces on a chessboard that no one knew existed, and each time there was a checkmate, Boss got a new toy. When the First Family took an overseas vacation, it was more than the Bench could brook.

By this time, the second and third asses, whose share of limelight had been eclipsed by Boss Hogg, picked up the static buzzing from the Bench, and thus throughout the town. They began to do some after-hours paper-shuffling, picked up a trail, and burned the midnight oil following the scent of something down that trail.

Can a small town keep its secrets? You bet it can. Better to take care of matters quietly. That's really how the sausage is made. It was never revealed what the second and third asses found on their hunting trip, but within a month of the First Family's return, the "statement" on Hogg's front lawn was gone, a lonely "For Sale" sign in its place.

Just like the Capitol cloakroom, the Bench dealt in scuttlebutt. Gossip is currency there, and information is power. Once the word came down that something was afoot up the road, there was a scurrying. The last thing an instigator wants is to have to shoulder any blame. The Bench was in total agreement that this whole matter be dealt with "in house." No sporting destination needed headlines having to do with embezzlement, or whatever it was that asses one and two had unearthed.

Be careful what you wish for, as the saying goes. Once Boss Hogg was gone, once those crop circles on his client's lawn were replaced by boring straight rows, the Bench went into a kind of slump. Only rumors of Boss's whereabouts fanned up a spark now and then. Some days it was a town in southern Maine, some days it was a whole new state. Though they'd be hard-pressed to admit it, the geezers missed their mayor. He'd kept them busy with a storyline that put a bounce in their gait. It was a tough transition for them when the speed of gossip slowed to a crawl. Was any part of the story (mostly of their own concoction) ever true? Or had they merely fabricated something to feed their bottomless appetite for scuttlebutt? Life on the Liar's Bench waxes and wanes with the talk of the town.

9

Evermore

Just before I sat down to write this story, two ravens landed on a pine limb outside the office window where I work. Shy and skittish by nature, this was unusual. They were actually close enough for me to see that peculiar turn at the tips of their beaks, enabling them to use it effectively as a tool for opening, grasping, cutting, and holding. I could also see that gothic black-feathered "hood" that comes down the face almost far enough to cover their eyes. Their heads turned this way and that as we stared at each other for several minutes. I mused to myself that they were here as editors to make sure I got this story right.

Spirits were running high for the group from North Carolina, a party of six in need of three guides. They'd practically had to buy separate plane seats for their tackle boxes, each of which was several tiers tall. These were anglers who attended sportsmen's shows and never walked away empty-handed. They packed every traditional and prototype lure into those drawers, with the rationale, "Something here's got to work!"

"You call this hot?" the patriarch of the group crowed on the first day. The temperature had already topped eighty by noon, and the guides were lamenting the hot summer. "This is a cool day in the Carolinas!" he laughed. "Hell, we stop fishin' in June and don't start up again till September— that's how hot it gets!" In recent years, more and more of our clientele hail from southern states.

On the second day, I was surprised when one of the guides, a man who is also one of my best friends, hadn't showed up at the lodge. He was always there before me. Then the third guide showed up with some news. The very worst news. My friend, a Native guide, wouldn't be coming in because his son had been killed overnight in a car accident after a graduation party. My blood stopped. I looked at my cell phone. I knew that, where I was standing, it wouldn't work. I raced for the kitchen of the lodge we were working out of, because there was a landline phone in there. When my friend picked up and I said his name, neither of us could speak for a moment. I searched desperately for something to say, but words failed me. Finally, I fumbled, "Tell me what to do. Just tell me." He said thanks, but there was really nothing. For now, he could only stay close to home with his wife and lie low. After we hung up, I just stood there, empty.

I walked off and found a rock to sit on where no one would see me. The image of the boy, Matthew, was crowding out every other thought, including that of going to work. My friend had groomed his son since toddlerhood to become an outdoorsman, savvy in all the traditional ways of the tribe, and now he was gone at the age of eighteen.

Girls his age used "cute" to describe him. The older women used "handsome." The men always said he was a good-looking boy. Actually, at eighteen, he was more man than boy.

When it came to his outdoor skills, none of his peers was his equal. His grandfather, an elder and a legend in the tribe, was still alive when Matthew was young, so that he learned not only from his father but from his father's father. His friends might look at a basswood hide stretcher in the Passamaquoddy museum and say, "What the hell is that?" But Matthew knew exactly what it was. He'd used them! Muskrat was still prized, especially by the elders of the tribe, for its tender, tasty meat, and also, in good years, for its cash value to vendors. By the time of his grandfather's passing, Matthew was already using the newer metal hide stretchers, as basswood was increasingly hard to come by.

In the woods, he was a natural. For at least fourteen years, he'd been learning more outdoor skills than most do in a lifetime. That's because, in his family's history, those skills had nothing to do with sporting and everything to do with survival. He learned at a young age to distinguish each game animal and furbearer's tracks in freshly fallen snow. The black bear, its signature five claws looking almost like crescent-shaped candy kisses, would've been unmistakable to him. He could even tell you why it sometimes appeared as if the beast had only two legs: to conserve energy, they'll sometimes step with their hind legs into the depression already made in the snow by their front legs. Where the differences between coyote tracks and dog tracks might elude the other kids his age, Matthew could explain it in very few words: the coyote print is oval, with sharp, pointy claws atop each toe, and they walk in a straight line. A dog's track is apt to be all over the place, rounder in shape, and with blunter claws, due to trimming and contact with hard surfaces.

His knowledge reached into the deep woods, where the secretive, larger buck deer kept vigil. He knew where they migrated in winter because his beaver trapping led him all over reservation lands, taking in the habits and movements of its wildlife. Had he not been killed in that terrible crash, he could have very easily, at eighteen, become a master guide that very summer, and joined us guiding sports who would've marveled at his skills.

On our last day of fishing, I took my two North Carolinians to the north end of Big Lake, which borders the Passamaquoddy reservation. My friend's house is on the lake, and, just as I thought, when we rounded the point that brought his home into view, I saw the smoke rising. It was from the fire that was started, according to tribal tradition, right after the tribal member had died. It is fed continuously right up to and through the completion of the burial, sometimes lasting a week or more. From a distance, I could see that my friend was sitting in a lawn chair, poking at the coals with a stick. I kept my distance, but when he turned, he saw me. Even from four hundred yards, he would know from the canoe, the motor, and the hat I wear, that it was me. He gave his trademark wave, in which he jackknifes his open palm up to his shoulder and back in a rapid-fire motion. I returned the wave and moved on, my heart aching from the image.

I kept reaching out to my friend and his wife, but they were as yet unable to talk, to move, barely to breathe. They had both invested everything they had in their boy, and now they were broken. My friend had recently refurbished a canoe for his son. The family had a camp on a remote stream, deep within tribal territory. Matthew knew his way around that country: where the best muskrat trapping could be found, where the beaver houses were for trapping in December, where to set up to call moose during their rut in October. Matthew was fishing before most of his peers. His father had taught him where the early spring brook trout were and what signs to look for to find the fiddlehead medallions along old stream beds where elms used to grow. They appeared at the same time of year, so every year after the age of ten, Matthew brought home a great charge of trout and fiddleheads for supper. He knew how to find white perch in late summer by catching one and attaching a small balloon or bobber to it, then following it all day as it kept up with the school. At fourteen, he could take two fillets off the fish as fast as a butcher brings his blade up and down a strop. A haul of forty fish would be done in twenty minutes. When he found baitfish and wanted to stay put and catch them without muddying up his anchor, he knew how to drive his paddle into the mud, tie it off to one gunwale of his canoe, and stay right there until he was ready to leave. When he and his friends took overnight camping trips, it was always Matthew who started the fires, even in the pouring rain; always Matthew who did all the cooking, especially when they were cooking fish or game they'd harvested that same day. To Matthew's friends, he was a guide already, confident and full of know-how for any situation that arose.

The tribal community went into mourning along with the family. Friends and neighbors parked on the street, then walked down to the lake where the fire was going and helped feed it. The weather never let up. An oppressive heat hung over the reservation and over the windless lakes. A grave was made during this heat, at the top of Cemetery Hill opposite the church, overlooking the waters of Long Lake after they pass through the narrows from Big Lake. It seemed there was always a pair of eagles soaring over that bay, then landing on giant pine limbs hanging out over the water on the other side. The Passamaquoddy word for eagle sounds in English like "jeep-log-ann." Matthew, like most of his tribe, took a worshipful view of the majestic raptor, which appeared in tribal art, crafts, woodworking, basket-making, and murals, as well as in traditional songs, prayers, and poems. The ancient symbolism was still alive and meaningful in the tribe.

The day was set for the funeral. It was exactly a week from the accident, on a Saturday. As soon as I found out, I grabbed my scheduling calendar and saw that it was my one day off in a two-week stretch of guiding jobs. The night before, there would be a gathering of friends and family at the home of Matthew's parents. By that time, according to tradition, the body would have been brought to the home and situated in the casket, facing east. Items of historic, personal, and family significance would be placed in the casket to accompany the deceased to the spirit world.

In the days leading up to the services, I guided a delightful family from Portland, Maine—a mom and dad and three sons. Martha, the mom, had not wanted to split everyone up, going off with different guides, so we kept the family together by going to my camp. From there, I could run a kind of taxi service, taking two out at a time while the others fished from shore, swam, or swung in the hammock, reading.

No one was more surprised than me when all three teenaged boys were able to catch salmon while trolling flies near the surface. In July! During a heatwave! It must have been due to the low cloud cover, mist, and fog, which will sometimes bring salmon up. But it was more than I ever expected. All the salmon were released, according to the boys' wishes, but we caught and kept several smallmouth bass for our lunch on our final day together. Gathered around the cook fire, Martha was visibly proud of her boys. They'd come with no tackle and very little experience with this kind of fishing, and yet they'd all managed to score the big prize everyone hopes for.

My wife had baked a batch of cream cheese brownies, and when she bought them out of the camp on a platter, the boys went silent, staring at them almost worshipfully. The next sound we heard was not of the human type, but of the corvid type—namely a raven's call. It falls somewhere between a screech and a word, though there are many variations of the sound—enough, in fact, to comprise a vocabulary. My wife and I were very familiar with the sound; the thing that was not familiar was a raven landing on a limb directly over the cook fire. They are an exceedingly shy and wary raptor, often taking wing over nothing more than a curtain or a door opening. Under normal circumstances, it is very difficult to get close to a raven. Apparently, these weren't normal circumstances.

When I said as much to our guests, all gazing up at the inky-black newcomer, the bird suddenly lifted off, and, instead of absconding as I expected, it dive-bombed Martha. She let out an involuntary scream and ducked her head. The raven never touched her, but its wingbeats blew a tuft of Martha's hair up. Then, instead of leaving, the raven resumed its post above the picnic area. I stared at it, dumbfounded. In a whole career of guiding, after seeing thousands of ravens, I'd never witnessed behavior so opposite to their character. As I tried to process what

I was seeing, the bird launched its second mission. This time, I watched carefully as the bird swooped down, and I noticed that it did not have its talons extended. If this were an attack, or if it was trying to steal food, the talons would be open and ready to grasp. Three times, four times, and then the huge bird landed in a tree farther off. Everyone was looking for an explanation. I had none. It's true that ravens love trinkets and all manner of shiny objects, and both Shelley and Martha were wearing ear hoops and perhaps a necklace. Still, this would not be enough for these corvids to overcome their timidity around humans, at least not in my experience. We sent Martha and her family on their way, with good stories to tell their friends back in Portland.

When my wife and I reached Matthew's home for the gathering of family and friends, we had to walk quite a ways, the neighborhood was so crowded with cars. Arriving, we walked around the house and headed for the lake. That's where the throng of people was, down by the fire that would not be allowed to go out until after the funeral. There were tables covered with food, some of it Native, like Indian bread, sometimes known as "fry bread," which is made with cornmeal, yeast, egg, and shortening. Matthew's relatives were all there, welcoming many people that they had never met. The mood was somber but intimate. At one point, I went to the house to use the bathroom and saw Matthew's mom in the kitchen, making coffee. We hugged for a long time, and, looking over her shoulder, I saw that she had a continuous loop of images playing across the TV screen. They were of her son, from babyhood to very recently. As everyone always said, it was hard to imagine a handsomer boy. I froze in place, watching the pictures of Matthew's fish and game adventures, his catches, his trophies, his joy in the outdoors. His mom was empty of tears, desolate. It was the way someone looked who had been crying for a week. I put anything I might have said into our hug instead.

When I returned to the gathering, I noticed that the women, my wife included, had moved themselves into a circle of lawn chairs. The men were nearer the fire, where I joined them. We talked of the heat, the fishing, water levels and game sightings, topics much more manageable than the sorrow beneath our words. We were there simply to be close. To feel something of Matthew because of his relationship to each of us. We shared everything we could when we couldn't share him.

As it grew dark and the summer assault of mosquitoes descended in force, we retreated to the house, where the images still played across the screen. The casket was closed, but my friend and guiding colleague, Matthew's father, told me about some of the items they'd placed inside. There was a miniature pair of snowshoes, woven from ash strips by his grandfather, whom he had loved so much and learned so much from. Also a tiny pack basket to hold his traps for his trapline in the spirit world. In fact, most of the items were miniature symbols of the skills Matthew had mastered in his short life in this world, there so that he might make use of them in the next.

On our way home, my wife was quiet and looked very pensive. After several miles, I asked what the women had talked about when they formed their circle. She said that Matthew's great aunt, Deanne, posed a question to the group. "Has anyone noticed the ravens acting strange lately?" My wife said her heart stopped. Having just come, the day before, from the strangest raven experience of her life, she couldn't believe what she was hearing. She was about to speak when several of the other women said "Yes," in unison. She was stunned again. Ravens perching on windowsills. Ravens outside a bedroom window, looking in. Sitting on a bird feeder on the deck. All these anomalies had been seen during the previous week by mostly Native women in the group, including Deanne, which is why she had brought it up. My wife said that Deanne, the oldest of the women, seemed the least surprised of all. She told them she'd seen this a couple of times before after an untimely death in the tribe. She said that, usually, everyone who had experienced this phenomenon had some relationship or connection with the deceased.

I knew what ravens meant in tribal traditions. They were revered for their wisdom, as message carriers, as guardians, as a first alert to danger, and much more. I'd taken an interest in them myself because of this, and yet nothing I'd read or experienced had prepared me for what I'd just heard, much less for what was yet to come.

The heat that had been oppressing northeastern Maine for so long lasted another day. The doors of the church were allowed to remain open to let air into the sanctuary. Women fanned themselves with the programs and anything else they could get their hands on. Men loosened their ties, took off their jackets, and mopped their brows with bandanas. The service in Passamaquoddy funerals is a combination of Catholic rites and rituals and Native custom. Incense was passed over the casket, which rested in the center aisle, in front of the podium where the priest stood with tribal elders behind him. There was also smudging of sweet grass, drumming, and singing, just as the tribe had done for centuries. It was difficult to make the ceremony a celebration of life when all people could think was how much life had been denied Matthew. Nevertheless, tradition was upheld, and after the last person spoke, the casket was bathed in smoke and then wheeled out of the church and into the street leading up to the cemetery. A long procession followed, sweltering in the mid-day July sun. At the top of the hill, a large circle formed around the burial site, closest family nearest the bier, then rows of people behind them. Here, there was more drumming, chanting, and singing, and then some final words from the parish priest. Once this was done, a relative of Matthew's took a shovelful of dirt from the mound next to the grave and held it out. The crowd then processed past, each person taking a handful of dirt and throwing it onto the casket. My friend and his wife stood, inconsolable, as people spoke to them, hugged them, cried with them. I said my piece to them and walked toward my truck. It was the saddest funeral I'd ever attended.

The combination of the heat and the weight of this sadness was almost unbearable. Afterward, all I could think of was the lake. When we reached the camp, my wife slumped into a rocker on the porch, but I got out of the truck and walked toward the water, disrobing with each step. My suit and tie and jacket lay on the ground behind me as I waded up to my waist and then dove under. It did nothing to mitigate the heaviness in my heart but everything to provide relief to every other overheated part of me. I dove deep, because that's where the water is always the coolest—close to the bottom. When I came up, I felt like I could breathe again, only now, the air wasn't so stifling. After treading water for several minutes, I finally turned around to head back, but noticed something on my dock that stopped me. I shook my head and blinked the water out of my eyes, but it was still there. A raven stood on the end of my dock between me and shore. I wanted to shout to my wife on the porch but knew it would spook the bird. In thirty years, I'd never seen a raven on that dock, or, for that matter, this close to me. I decided to move closer. At first, the raven didn't move; it just kept turning its head this way and that, looking at me with one eye, then the other. I made an effort not to splash or make a ruckus as I gradually approached the giant bird. When I was a scant ten feet away, the raven turned, made two or three hops until it lighted on a boulder, then turned around again. I stopped. The starring contest resumed. I began to move forward. This time, the bird let me get even closer. When something told me that on my next step it would take off, I took the step anyway. It hopped once, opened its wings, but landed on a limb only twenty feet away. When it landed, it turned and looked directly at me, just the way it had been doing all along. It had never made a sound, and neither had I.

Finally, I couldn't help myself. Whether it was to learn what this raven's business was about, or merely to confront something that would be impossible for anyone to believe later, I opened my mouth and said, "Matthew?" The bird waited two seconds, then answered, but not with its trademark, "Quark!" It was some other sound, possibly well within the raven's substantial repertoire of sounds, which to us is noise, but to them is language. If it was an English word, I could not discern it. Only later did it occur to me that it might have been a Passamaquoddy word. Either way, the confrontation had a strong effect. As I stood there, my suit clothes lying on the ground in front of me, the crushing sadness I'd felt before plunging into the lake was gone.

Rather than insist on an immediate answer to this mystery, I decided to just let it be what it was and see what shape it took as time went on. In the several years since Matthew's passing, I've never had another raven experience remotely like that one. I've certainly continued to see them, sometimes to feed them, and I have sometimes even tried to speak to them. I've never gotten as close again, nor have I ever received a response, despite my attempts. As is so often the case, in time, it came to me that the explanation for what had happened wasn't a matter of either this or that. Perhaps the incident I'd had with the raven was simply an opening. Experiences like these were foreign to my culture and upbringing. Our programmed response is to be dismissive, using labels like "occult" or "wacky." Not so for Matthew or his father. They didn't visit the natural world occasionally, for recreational or sporting purposes. They *were* that world, in sync with its rhythms, its subtleties, and its language. The raven behavior that Deanne had first brought up among the women at the gathering had been witnessed by people who all had one thing in common: a close relationship to the deceased. If belief could be elastic enough to embrace the idea of communication with the spirit world, then it would follow that that communication might take different forms. The raven, venerated as it was in the tribe for its wisdom and intelligence, might be a likely candidate.

It proved rewarding to let an idea like that take shape on its own over time. Rewarding because it did produce an opening. Since then, I've paid closer attention to the languages, rhythms, and subtleties around me as I move through the natural world.

I'd been missing too much! Since then, I've made sure to be listening whenever Matthew has something to say.

10

Shop Party

When I was starting out as a guide, I was lucky enough to get invited to a shop party in town at which all of the oldest guides would be present.

What is a shop party? Most guides, trappers, canoe makers, and bait dealers have a shop somewhere on their property. There is likely some order of workbench in there, probably with a vise or two attached to it. Tools might be hung behind and above it, traps or snowshoes hang on spikes driven into studs and rafters, and there are drawers, plenty of drawers, for screws, nails, and all types of fasteners. Either a potbelly or ram-down stove will heat the work area. There will also be a hiding place or two, known only to the shop owner. This is for the new pair of waders that the wife doesn't know he purchased, and by the time they come out in the spring, she'll think he's had them all along. This hiding place is also safe harbor for spirits reserved for special occasions, the definition of which may vary from strict to lax.

By any measure, this shop party was truly special. Names that were steeped in local legend suddenly had faces. And not only that; they had stories to tell. The host in whose shop the party took place was, with the permission of all in attendance, videotaping the event. You might worry that the cameras would be off-putting to these technology-deprived old guides. It was one thing to have their "pitcher took," but quite another to be in the movies. This fear proved unfounded. Used to holding court with sports under every imaginable condition, used to entertaining, telling stories, and even improvising at times, these fellows rose to the camera like a salmon to an elk hair caddis fly.

I was the interloper, there by the grace of my friend Jack Perkins, the host. I had nothing to contribute but my full attention and, much of the time, my belly-laughter. What I noticed first was the timing and delivery, which seemed to come naturally to all these titans of the trade. The tales were filled with detail, and deliciously exasperating for the way they stalled the story and kept you in suspense. Where had they learned that? Were they born that way?

Another aspect of their art form was that, in the end, it didn't matter to you whether the story was true or false. You were so enchanted, drawn into it so completely, watching as it grew to some unforeseen fruition, that it would never occur to you to ask. Embellishment surely has to be one of the cardinal tools of this brand of storytelling. The truth is certainly back there somewhere; something did in fact happen, and the story you're hearing is certainly based upon that. If you wanted to, you could try and separate fact from fiction, but if you were the type for whom that was necessary, you probably wouldn't have been invited to this shop party in the first place.

I'll recount just two tales, partly because they so intrigued me, but also because to tell more might be overstepping some invisible line of propriety. Some of the material was highly personal, and all of the men in that room save the host are now gone.

T.O.M.

Like most people in town, I'd heard anecdotes from the Texas oil man's (Tom's) tale, but had never heard the whole thing. The fellow had come from Midland, Texas, home of presidents and petroleum moguls. In Texas, he may have been recognized, lionized, even feared for his power and influence due to his mega-conquests, and he seemed to expect the same obsequiousness everyplace else. The problem was that, to a guide, a client is a client. You can't categorize them according to how successful they've been. The only decent thing to do is treat everyone fairly, trying to pick up on their skill levels and gently bringing them along from there. And a good guide keeps in mind that the end game is always fun.

Tom made it clear upon his arrival that he already knew everything related to fishing, a veteran fishing guide's worst nightmare. Even though he was new to Grand Lake Stream, he would fish his way, and catch fish on his terms. As it turned out, his guide, Alo, was a Native American guide working out of the same lodge where Tom was staying. Alo's ancestors, as far back as the tribe's oral history goes, had all been guides. He'd gone with his dad from the time he could stand on a dock. All of the interconnecting waters around the Passamaquoddy Reservation were his domain. He knew when certain fisheries "turned on" in the spring, and exactly where to be on those bodies of water when they did. Tom didn't know how lucky this luck of the draw was until he lost it.

This particular storyteller at the shop party was smoking a thick black cigar from one end, and chewing it from the other. Watching this, you couldn't help wondering which would win, the chewing end or the burning end. The man was talking around his cigar, something he'd clearly had years to perfect. As I wasn't used to his garbled speech, I'll pass along the best translation I can from having watched the video several times.

Tom came out of the lodge on the first morning wearing a kind of white paste on his face, as if he'd just performed in a minstrel show. He also wore a huge, broad-brimmed straw hat. Alo was familiar with face paint, but only ceremonially when the tribe had its annual "Indian Days" celebration. Tom didn't fit that bill, so Alo reasoned it had to be some kind of sunblock. "Allergic" was the first word of the day out of Tom's mouth, apparently feeling obligated to explain, albeit succinctly. "Oh," Alo said. He'd seen some folks who were allergic to the sun wearing scarves, broad-brimmed straw hats, and various lotions, but never a thick, white paste quite like this one. Alo couldn't decide whether the man looked more like a mime or a clown.

The thing the Native guide noticed most about Tom, besides the minstrel paste, was his gait. It vaguely resembled someone trying to walk with splints on both legs. Tom caught him looking. "Arthritis," he snarled. "Oh," Alo replied. Other than these, the only other words Tom uttered were, "Let's go!"

But not just yet. One awkward incident stalled their departure from the lodge. When Tom got to the guide's truck, he reached into his pocket, came up with a small camera, and handed it over. Fair enough. Most sports want to capture different moments of their adventure, and apparently Tom wanted a photo of the beginning. But when he backed up to the driver's-side door of Alo's truck, he was suddenly yanked backward and plastered up against it as though he'd been pushed. "Magnets," he growled, apparently a man of one-word outbursts rather than sentences. "Oh?" Alo asked, not fully understanding what he meant. "Arthritis," he snipped. "A hand?"

The shop was already humming with muffled laughter. The billionaire from Midland wore special magnets in his clothing, which were supposed to alleviate the pain of his arthritis, which was everywhere in his body. He was stuck to the truck like a leech to Humphrey Bogart in *The African Queen*. Alo reached for his hands but was unable to free him that way. Tom screeched in pain when he tried, but he wouldn't come loose. Alo regrouped. "Both hands," the oil man snapped, so Alo reached for both of his hands again. "No! Around me," Tom barked. Only then did Alo realize what this cranky customer was asking. He'd have to give the sport a full-frontal hug and try to pull him away from the truck. It worked. Such was the intimate start of the not-so-intimate adventure that was to follow. The brandy that had come out of the secret shop drawer had begun its travels from hand to hand at this point.

That morning, after checking the wind direction and the weather, Alo had already decided where to go. Grand Falls Flowage, which is really the West Branch of the St. Croix River system, was his destination. It had been fishing very well of late, and he was seeing a lot of larger fish. It was buggy, but so was everyplace else. It was early June, and blackflies had begun their annual vampiric predations on any available blood. As usual, they seemed to prefer the out-of-state kind. When Tom got out of Alo's truck at Squirrel Point, the public boat launch, he immediately jumped back in. Alo reached into his possibles bag and came up with a can of Deep Woods OFF! He brandished it to Tom, who shouted back at him, "Allergic!" Alo reached back in and came up with a mosquito net to be worn over the head. Tom impatiently shook his head, "No!"

"Stay here till I get launched," the Native guide said through the window. "When we get underway in the canoe it'll be better." It was, but only until they stopped. It took twenty minutes or so for the blackflies to find them, and only another five before Tom took the head net that had been offered. He didn't like it, claimed he couldn't see well enough with it on, and therefore it became a convenient scapegoat for not catching any fish. The man was having a bad morning. Gently, gingerly, Alo tried making suggestions: spray some Deep Woods on his clothing or on his hat. He refused, on account of his allergy. When he showed exasperation over his lack of success, Alo extended his arm to hand him his silver bullet lure. Tom waved it off. He needed no one telling him how to catch fish. Nevertheless, he grew more and more agitated as the morning progressed.

"Look," he began, after an hour of frustration. "You're not putting me over the fish. Do that now so I can stop wasting my time." Alo swallowed hard. He thought of pulling out the collapsible rod hidden under his seat and then showing the rude guest a fish or two. Stretching his elastic patience a little further, he overcame the temptation. Instead, he started the motor and moved to a second hotspot he knew well. There, the testy oil titan began a feverish barrage of rapid-fire casting, using a largemouth bass lure that worked perfectly well on the man-made bass ponds of west Texas.

"Listen," he said through the mosquito net after lashing the lake for fifteen minutes. "I don't think you heard me. I came a long way, and I'm paying good money. Are you hearing me now?" Alo was, but it would take more than this to make him reach his boiling point. If that ever did happen, which was rare, then a new name would be added to the short list in what everyone in the shop knew as "Alo's Black Book." In it were the names of people who'd found a way through Alo's indefatigable good nature, and now the ill-tempered Texan was showing promise.

Dutifully, Alo started up the motor once again and headed for Dinner Island. There were rocky shoals and ancient stumps in that area, a place he sometimes reserved for the end of the day to give his clients a big finish to remember. Also, he'd be close to the lunch ground for which Dinner Island was named. The one camp on the small island, owned at the time by a couple from Connecticut, had a fire pit and picnic table next to a small landing that they allowed local guides to use.

Still in a foul mood, Tom ripped off the head net, changed lures again to something Alo was sure he'd seen on a cable TV fishing show, and began madly flinging it toward the first shoal. "Goddamnit!" he bellowed. He was hung up. Alo hated to paddle right into the shoal and ruin the fishing there, so he asked for the rod.

"Look," Tom fired back at him. It was at this point that Alo suddenly remembered something. The several names in his little Black Book all seemed to share one thing in common. They all tended to begin their sentences with either "Look" or "Listen." Presumably, this meant that whatever you were about to hear was the definitive truth from an unimpeachable source. The real intention, however, was to put you in your place. Alo smiled, still reaching for the man's rod. When at last he gave it up, Alo held it high, trapped the monofilament line against the butt section of the rod, then pulled out line with the other hand as though the rod were a longbow. The cantankerous sport snickered, surely thinking this was some Indian stunt that was supposed to impress him. After pulling the line out, Alo let it go while simultaneously whipping the tip of the rod forward, creating slack in the line all the way to the lure. At the right moment, he pulled up, and the lure was free. Alo reeled up and handed the rod back to his sport, who showed no sign of being either impressed or grateful.

It was a rare day indeed when Alo brought a sport into a lunch ground without so much as a perch or a pickerel to fry up as an hors d'oeuvres. He would never say so to the blustery Texan, but the smallmouth bass in our local lakes are so accommodating that even small children seldom get skunked.

Tom needed help getting out of the canoe, and he'd worn leather-soled loafers for a fishing adventure to Maine. Seeing this, and perhaps invoking Sir Walter Raleigh's chivalry in laying down his cloak to keep the queen's feet dry, Alo set a boat cushion in the shallow water beside the canoe where Tom would step out, but he bobbled and got wet anyway. "Goddamnit!" he yelled, as if this was Alo's fault. And maybe that's when Alo recalled that the same queen Sir Walter Raleigh coddled had him beheaded shortly thereafter.

Everyone hearing the story in the shop knew of Alo's legendary long temper, slow fuse, and dry wit. With another sport, Alo might've sought to bring some levity at this point by asking, "So how was your morning?" but he could already see that this was one of those cases where the more you stir, the worse it stinks. And sure enough, bad was about to turn worse. A cloud of blackflies that impressed even Alo descended onto Dinner Island. When he realized Tom had been without his bug net ever since getting hung up, he rushed to the canoe to find it. It was gone. It must've gone over the side when Tom ripped it off.

When Alo returned, he decided not to bring it up. He worked fast to get a fire going, using lots of birch bark for a good smudge of smoke to fog the flies. He looked in the lunch basket from the lodge and found two raw steaks wrapped in newspaper inside an ice pack, and potatoes and onions in a plastic bag. Working as fast as he could, he started chopping those up, only occasionally glancing over to the picnic table where Tom was seated. His white paste having faded, he was applying a new coat. Unfortunately, the stuff had no effect as a repellant. Welts began to appear on his forehead. "Mosquito net!" he demanded. His vocabulary suffered from a "please and thank you" deficit, but Alo explained that the net must've gone over the side when Tom had taken it off. He was sorry—he didn't have another. Alo watched that projectile hit its mark. When it did, the irascible billionaire with a fresh coat of paté on his face pushed himself up from his seat and glared at Alo.

"Listen here, my little Indian," he began, and he might as well have stopped right there, because Alo didn't hear whatever came next. With a smile on his face, he calmly stood, walked down to his canoe, lifted up the bow, stepped one foot in, and shoved off with the other. "Hey!" the vexed Texan yelled after him. But Alo, taking his seat and looking right at him, still smiling, feathered a few backward paddle strokes, turned, and started the motor. Now Tom was on his feet, shouting something, but his guide revved the engine and never heard what it was.

This part got the shop brandy moving even faster, until one of the old guides held it up empty. "No worries," said the host as he stood and went into his "safe." The smoking end and the chewing end of the speaker's stogie had finally met in the middle. Now, without it, you could understand what he was saying.

"Alo never went far," the storyteller started up again. He went back and started casting those shoals within sight of Dinner Island—the ones they'd just left. In fact, he found the mosquito net there, floating just under the surface. Everybody could picture exactly where Alo was, his irate oil man on shore watching him as he boated fish after fish. When it was a particularly impressive one, Alo took his time, making sure to hold it up high to inspect it thoroughly before gently releasing it over the side. He calmly fished for an hour, and the whole time he could almost feel the blood boiling on shore, those two angry eye slits, encased in paste, glowering at him. He was careful not to look directly at Tom, but out of his peripheral vision, he could see him swatting, thrashing, and slapping himself futilely against a biblical onslaught of blackflies that took to their victim's blood like Tom took to Texas crude.

When Alo thought that the point had been sufficiently made, instead of starting the outboard, he slowly paddled over to the island. Tom, clearly in distress, cowered at the picnic table. When the bow of Alo's canoe was twenty feet from shore, Tom stood up. "I'm sorry," he said, and Alo took another slow paddle stroke. When he heard his hull touch bottom, he stood, walked forward, stepped out of the canoe, and looked at his sport, a sorry sight. One eye was swollen shut, the other, almost. Knobs rose up all over his face and skull. The only thing Alo could think of was the Elephant Man. Tom's head size had ballooned so much that he couldn't get his straw hat to stay on. After taking all this in, Alo said, "OK then," and walked past Tom to pick up the lunch basket. He and his wife would have steaks for dinner, back on the reservation.

Tom didn't ask to fish on the ride back to the landing, but he was a transformed person, meek and penitent in every sinew and ligament. At the launch, he asked Alo if he would show him the lure he was using in the shoal water that afternoon, and he said "please." Instead of showing him the lure that was on the rod, Alo reached into his tackle box, found a new one, still in its package, and handed it to Tom. "Hang on to that one," he said. Tom looked down at it, then back up at Alo. "Thank you." Tom's vocabulary had expanded.

Back at the lodge, the Native guide was careful not to let the tycoon stick to the truck again, as he was not in the mood for another hug. Suddenly, Tom reached out his hand to Alo. In it was a three hundred-dollar tip. "I'm sorry again for my behavior." Alo nodded and tipped his hat, seeing that his sport was indeed sorry. Perhaps he'd been too used to servile, slavish behavior in the people who worked for him. Perhaps no one had ever dared teach him a lesson, and it was only this that won his respect. Whatever the case might have been, once in his truck, Alo reached into the center console, pulled out a black leather-bound notebook, and wrote, "Clown face," to commemorate one sport who would certainly be forgiven but never forgotten.

SILAS

The Old Trapper, Earl Bonness, himself a natural raconteur, was there with us in the shop, feeling forty-something instead of eighty-something by this time. He could vamp in front of a camera with the best of them. So, when he decided to tell the story of the hippie that came to town in 1972, everyone but me knew exactly who he was talking about—the tape shows them all smiling broadly. They also looked pleased for the excuse to get that bottle moving again.

Apparently, the only things that had marked Silas as a hippie to Grand Lake Stream, which hadn't yet seen one in the flesh, were his shoulder-length blond hair, and the fact that he went everywhere barefoot—to the store, to the post office, even to town meeting. When there were pickup or even league softball games on the ball field in the center of town, he always played barefoot. Surely that had to be a hippie!

The Old Trapper said he was a "friendly cuss" all the same. "And you talk about smart!" Earl threw in. With his own background, it would have taken a lot to impress him, but Silas had evidently managed that. He'd been addicted to the outdoors ever since childhood somewhere in southern Maine. Earl told the camera in his trademark soft-spoken manner that Silas owned a massive collection of traps, his own homemade snowshoes, muskrat stretchers, a hide-tanning setup in his shop, as well as an arsenal of hunting rifles. Earl painted a picture of a very familiar way of life in Grand Lake Stream, one that everyone in the room had lived at one time or another.

From the day he arrived in town, Silas, rather than looking for a career position that didn't exist, began to stitch together a living. Like everyone listening, this lifestyle seemed to agree with him. Living according to somebody else's clock didn't suit Silas any more than it did Earl's audience in the shop. So that first winter, he mail-ordered some redworms from a farm in Arkansas and began to grow and multiply them in long, narrow boxes covered with burlap. He kept the dark, rich soil mixture moist by sprinkling water onto the burlap. He fed his worms coffee grinds, which Silas said had the effect of increasing reproduction. Earl paused here, allowing the idea of caffeine-inspired worm rutting to settle over his listeners. He also gave a knowing nod to the camera. Amid all the whiskers and chawing jaws, little grins showed up around the room.

Come spring, Silas had an inventory of trout worms that would last through June, at which time they would become bass worms. His investment paid for itself within the first week. It took very little, Earl said, to keep Silas in beans, and this was only one of the means he employed.

Another made use of a skill he'd been honing since grade school. "Turns out," Earl said, "he was awful handy with leather." That was what had inspired his tanning setup in the first place. Much of what Silas wore in winter was leather, the one exception being the gum rubber boots he had on his feet every waking hour during cold weather. His skills at keeping his own gear in good shape developed into doing repairs for others. If you gave Silas a forty-year-old pair of snowshoes with dry-rotted bindings, he'd return them to you looking as if they'd come from the L.L. Bean catalog store in Freeport. And this leather work naturally overlapped into cobbling. He could stitch leather to rubber; in fact, he could stitch leather to almost anything. He came up with a door lock pouch that would protect padlocks from icing up in winter. It was the perfect solution to an age-old problem of not being able to get your key into a lock.

Obviously, Silas was deliberative and thoughtful in his enterprises. Within a year of his arrival, small change from his various skills added up to the dollars he needed to cover rent, fuel, and the supplies for his many trades. But even the sum of all these income-producers was a pittance next to what his traplines produced. Here was where his real genius lay. Furs of all types were fetching good money at that time, and whenever the truck from Montreal came to collect the spoils of working trappers, Silas's trove eclipsed all the others combined.

Skilled outdoorsmen can be a jealous lot, covetous of their methods, and ruffled when someone else's proves superior. More importantly, a new whiz kid always gets the attention of game wardens, who reason, "No one is that good. He must be going outside the law." But this reasoning was flawed when applied to Silas, something the game wardens would soon learn at their own expense. The Old Trapper was the perfect person to be telling this story to the video camera, and to a shop full of his contemporaries. His historic rivalry with an old game warden from bygone days named Darky White was by this time mythology. Also, from the way he was telling the story, you got the impression that he had a soft spot for Silas, even if he was a hippie.

Seasons for trapping furbearers are denoted clearly in the law book. Many of them overlap, so that a trapper is simultaneously setting out traps for a variety of species: bobcat, coyote, fox, mink, muskrat, opossum, otter, raccoon, red squirrel, pine marten, skunk, weasel, and fisher cat. And that's not to mention the bigger payday: beaver. But sometimes a season ends and a trapper "forgets" to take up a few of his sets. Or sometimes he may appear to be trapping for one thing, when in reality he's after something else, the pelt price for which is climbing.

A buzz developed that Silas was doing too well. Something had to be amiss. Chatter set in, a sometimes-ominous matter in small towns. Game wardens are trained to tune in to chatter. They form friendships with locals who become surrogate ears to the ground. These huge harvests of premium pelts put something in the craw of Silas's competitors. It was only a matter of time, and the clock was ticking.

District Warden Bob Black had shown up around this time, brand new to the region. Up to then, the staying power of a new warden was about three years, and the reason for his inevitable departure was always the same: the wife. It was impossible to keep a warden at this remote outpost unless his wife had grown up here. Once the wife of a new warden discovered where she really was, hours from anything resembling the civilization she was used to, it was either the move or the marriage, and many a marriage had washed up on those shoals. Indeed, this would happen to the new district warden in question, but the demise of his wedlock was still a couple of years away.

The first thing he did was make it a point to meet Silas someplace public. He began to be frequently visible in town, especially by the big game scale outside the store, which, in the fall, was a magnet for local hunters and trappers. The warden had no problem spotting Silas, his long blond locks hanging down below his Mad Bomber hat, leather chaps over torn jeans, and his trademark gum rubbers on his feet. Warden Black came on strong, all teeth and handshakes. "Call me Bob," he told Silas, who immediately picked up an "off" scent on the officer. At this point, the Old Trapper paused, looked at the "video machine," and said, "And that's saying something if you ever smelled a trapper in the fall.

Soon, Silas began to see little signs: tire tracks beside his vehicle on logging roads or skidder trails, footprints running briefly along his trapline. He was being stalked, and perhaps worse, set up. In fairness, no local trappers, disgruntled as they might have been, did anything to aid and abet Warden Black, but nor did they do anything to dissuade him. The warden, reading the disgruntlement of Silas's competition, imagined that he was onto something big. The offender might even be working for a ring that was selling commercially. He contacted his superiors in Augusta for permission to use additional wardens for what promised to be a major takedown. A hippie trapper, possibly with help, was harvesting far beyond the norm, and it would take more than one law enforcement officer to crack the case. If all went well, such a triumph in his first year at his new post would bode favorably on his resume.

Soon after the warden's request to the higher-ups, three men posing as deer hunters checked into Indian Rock Camps. It didn't take Silas long to spot them as imposters. A real outdoorsman can pick out a desk jockey no matter how good an actor he might be. Then, a couple of times, Silas caught a glimpse of Warden Black in his truck with three other men. The stage was set.

The Old Trapper told us we were about to find out just how "clevah" Silas was. He immediately set to work laying out a new trapline in a very specific area. It was a nasty beaver swamp, the worst in the region, known to all present. Each of his beaver sets was clearly labeled, all on the up and up according to the law. They were set with poplar sticks as bait; the only difference was that Silas had removed the pan and trigger, the mechanism for actually catching the beaver. His reasoning here was two-fold. One was humor. He knew the wardens were following him, so he set a trap for them instead of the beavers. When they saw the triggerless traps, though there was nothing illegal about this, they'd be completely flummoxed and begin to suspect they were being played. The other was to show off his skill at decoying the wardens into deep trouble. The totally legal trapline took a circuitous route through some of the worst trudging this rough country has to offer. Silas left ample clues to make it obvious where the trapline began, and a discarded soda can here and there to delineate its route.

Since beavers are nocturnal and diurnal (active both day and night), most trappers tended their traps in the morning, leaving them reset for the remainder of the day and night. Long before the clandestine team of wardens had staked out Silas's trapline, he'd staked *them* out. The three "deer hunters" staying at Indian Rock Camps drove out of town each day, met up with Warden Black, then got into his truck. They waited till midday, then made a phone call back to town, where a cooperative snitch confirmed to them that Silas's truck was back, parked outside his house. Then off they went, into the boondocks, searching for the start of Silas's trap line. They were confident that, when they found it, it was going to be a big day, the kind of day a rookie warden might dream of.

Finally, the day came. When they got the go-ahead from town that Silas was back, the four men easily found the beginning of Silas's decoy trap line. They all bailed out of the truck in hot pursuit.

Soon after, when Silas's truck disappeared from his driveway, the unknown informer tried to call the wardens, but it was no use. They had left the truck in haste, and the warden's satellite phone was locked inside. They'd brought hip boots, hand saws, and cameras, but one hundred yards in, they wished they'd brought chest waders and winches. When they finally came to the first site, clearly and legally marked, they figured it was a fluke when they found no trap attached. A lucky beaver had probably made off with it, clamped to some part of its body. They pressed on, slogging great distances between marked trap sites. The going got only rougher, and by the time they reached the fifth site with no trap, the first hint of an awful truth dawned on them: they'd been duped. And worse, they now had to make the slog back through hell to get to the truck. Their hip boots filled up with water. Mud caked up on them, adding weight to every step. Not one of them had brought in so much as a bottle of water or a candy bar, so confident were they that this would be short work. Hours later, when the sun was going down, dehydrated and exhausted, they came within sight of the truck, a sweet relief. Until they got closer that is, and saw that all four tires were flat.

Earl wasn't about to let the brandy go past him again. Grabbing it and raising the bottle high, he said, "To Silas," and then took a "twitch," as he liked to call it. The grizzled group in the shop, right along with the Old Trapper, knew and respected Silas. They all knew that he eventually married a Native woman who seemed to understand him well, especially the wild part of him. Eventually, the tribe, recognizing his natural instincts in the woods and on the waters, made him a game warden. He earned a reputation for restraint, especially when hunger and poverty came into the equation.

The time stamp on the video indicates that the storytelling session lasted an hour and forty-five minutes. That must have been when the two bottles worth of memories had run out. No matter which, Jack Perkins owns the distinction of hosting the last known gathering of its kind in Grand Lake Stream, and of having the wisdom to preserve it for posterity. You can see some of these old guides cocking their heads to put their better ear closer to the speaker. Most had spent a life beside an outboard motor and had the compromised hearing to prove it. Later Jack, with one good ear himself, told me that, oftentimes, two old guides with one bad ear each could team up to hunt deer in the fall and overcome the hearing deficit. Since they both had the same deaf ear, they'd simply stand back-to-back, thereby achieving a 360-degree range of hearing.

Seeing Jack's shop full of these guiding titans, you wish Rockwell Kent had been present, painting this last great assembly. He'd capture the wool shirts and khaki pants, the deeply furrowed brows under the felt hats, pipe smoke billowing above their heads. And though he couldn't paint the laughter, you could still hear it just by looking at their faces. He might call the work, "The Back of Beyond: A Place out of Time." Or maybe just "Shop Party."

11
Just Another Mystery

Micah and I started fishing together when he was eleven. He's now twenty-seven, and we still do two trips per year together.

When he came that first year, he was a blank slate, brand new to fishing, which meant there were no bad habits to undo. I soon saw that he was a "show me" kind of learner, and a very quick study at that. But even as he started hooking and landing feisty smallmouth bass, one thing never changed on that first morning. Micah didn't speak.

I knew from his dad that he'd been adopted, along with his twin sister, from Peru. They were Inca. When I first guided Micah, I'd just read *1491*, by Charles C. Mann, and was thoroughly enthralled by the pre-Colombian accomplishments of the Inca people. They mastered self-government, achieved engineering feats that wouldn't be matched for centuries, and established a culture that is still visible at Machu Picchu, in the Andes Mountains of south-central Peru.

Naturally, I assumed there was a language barrier between Micah and myself, so I relied heavily on visible signals and gestures. I was amazed at how accurate his casts were within the short span of that first morning. His go-to lure turned out to be the Devil Horse, a torpedo-shaped tube in different colorful patterns, some imitating yellow perch, some white perch, and some various shiners. Micah's favorite was the yellow perch imitation. It had three sets of treble hooks suspended from the bottom of the lure, and two propellers, one at each end. This product, from the lure manufacturer that shares its name with the makers of a great Irish beer—Smithwick—never seems to stop working as some lures do when fish are over-exposed to them year after year. For one thing, it causes a lot of commotion on the surface. Bass respond to commotion, whether out of curiosity, excitability, or the possibility of a feeding frenzy. Micah learned to throw the lure to a target and then do absolutely nothing. Not knowing whether he was understanding me or not, I said we should think of it from the fish's point of view. Something new has landed from that other, non-liquid world, smack dab into our space. So, I said, let's give them time to study it.

And they do just that. Oftentimes, a smallmouth bass or a pickerel will lie under a lure, feathering its fins while looking at it. Then the lure moves. And when the Devil Horse moves, it does so with great fanfare and flourish. A very high percentage of the time, that's when the strike comes. The hardest part is the waiting after it splashes down. But Micah had no bad habits, nothing to unlearn. The first time it happened was a teaching moment, a gift that kept on giving for almost twenty years. Micah has mastered the patience it takes to draw that strike and then close the deal.

To my surprise, Micah was even happier when it was a pickerel that struck the lure, then fought all the way to the net, instead of a bass. The first time he caught one, I held it up after disgorging the hook and, with hand signals, asked him if he'd like to eat it. The wide grin was my answer.

Two of Micah's brothers and his dad were also on that trip, and when they brought bass in for the first course of their shore lunch, Micah simply held up his pickerel. They all looked at each other curiously. Pickerel have not earned the bad name that has been unfairly bestowed upon them. People blame them for being bony, forgetting that some of the world's most succulent delicacies come from creatures whose anatomies make harvesting their meat a challenge. Lobsters, blue crabs, American shad, and oysters all belong to that category. They all require a method, and likewise, the chain pickerel, one of the most unsung species in the songbook of anglers, does too.

Like so many of the tricks of the guiding trade, this one too is borrowed from our predecessors, Native guides. Many years ago, I sat at a picnic table next to legendary Passamaquoddy guide David Sockabasin while he slowed his usual speed at cleaning a pickerel so I could see and learn. With a razor-sharp Barlow knife, he scaled the fish first. Then, with precision cuts, he removed the dorsal fin, which, on pickerel, is located three-quarters of the way to the tail. David flipped the fish, in order, I assumed, to eviscerate it. Wrong. Instead, he turned his blade sideways and, while pressing it down along the spine, removed the entire underside of the pickerel. This, he told me, was where most of the offending bones were. When that was done, he removed the head and tail. All of this, up to this point, had been done in his hands, without ever setting the fish down on the table. Only now did he lay the thoroughly cleaned pickerel belly-side down (where the belly had been). Now, he carefully made slits perpendicular to the spine across the meat, pressing down until his blade touched bone. These incisions were about a half-inch apart when he was done.

This was what Micah watched, sitting beside me at a lunch ground on Sysladobsis Lake, following it through every phase: from cleaning into a wet mix, then a dry mix, then into the hot oil in a long-handled Greenfield frying pan. Micah's expression was fulfillment enough for me. He beamed proudly, as if he were nurturing his catch through the whole process of becoming edible. Once it was in front of him, the rest of the world was blotted out. Slowly, methodically, he addressed himself to each morsel in a kind of worshipful way that raised goosebumps on my skin.

When that meal was concluded, I stepped up to the table, coffee pot in hand. I'd already distributed double fudge and cream cheese brownies to the whole group. When I got to Micah, he shoved his blue enamel coffee cup up under the spout. I looked at his dad, who gave an approving nod, then filled Micah's cup to the brim. He added nothing to it.

I don't think I spoke a word for the rest of that day in the canoe. It was Micah who did all the talking, his English flawless. Apparently the taste of pickerel loosened his tongue, or else all he needed to stimulate locution was a cup of guide's coffee. I imagined his father and his brothers laughing in the other canoes. The joke was on me. Even so, I resolved from then on to steer Micah toward the haunts of pickerel whenever possible.

It was inevitable that, one day, after watching his father fly fish for so many years, Micah would pick up a fly rod himself. Once again, the learning curve for Micah was so short as to look more like a straight line, as though the language and grace of the movements were agreeable to Micah's body, already imprinted in his muscle memory.

Our fishing travels have brought us a long way over twenty years' time. Of the eleven interconnecting bodies of water in the immediate Grand Lake Stream area, we certainly have fished nine of them, and then have gone outside the area and fished more. He's a fisherman now, not a wannabe or a novice. He does his own thinking, reads the water himself, decides on lures or flies, and can delineate targets on his own. We've seen a lot of things together, memories that we share as companions on the water. We've seen moose swim by the canoe within a paddle's length, then hit the shore at a dead run. We've watched groups of otters, with their puppy dog faces, out-fishing us, so that we finally had to surrender and move on. The truth is that Micah doesn't really need a guide anymore. It may be that we just love hanging out together.

Nothing we'd ever seen, however, compared to the day when we went by canoe to the northernmost tip of Washington County, Maine. It's true that you can keep going by water and cross into another county with totally different regulations. But on this day, we stayed in Washington County to fish what is sometimes called an "arm," which is nothing but an extension of a larger lake.

It was June, the peak of the smallmouth spawning season, and the fish were shouting at us from every shore. The sun lit up the circles on the sandy bottom, each one with a dark center, each one with a male smallmouth vigilantly patrolling its perimeter. Micah was in fine form, first with spinning gear, then with the fly rod. The wind was down; the surface was a glass tabletop. These waters are gin-clear. You can easily see all the way to the bottom in depths up to twenty feet. If we're able to see the fish that well, they're surely able to see us. This forces anglers to make the perfect cast on the first try, because several misses will eliminate that particular spawning bed as a viable target: the male bass guarding it becomes too skittish. Not that this was a challenge for Micah. We'd released a dozen beauties, including a couple of trophies, before we'd made it all the way down one side of the arm.

Once in a while, on a day like this—mill-pond calm—a guide can stand up in the canoe for a better view. We'd just fished one of those Stonehenge-like boneyards of boulders sticking up at odd angles, and Micah had scored his lunch pickerel there. Now we were passing across an area of muddy bottom and rotting logs from the old pre-dam days when most of this body of water was a forest. This was not good habitat for spawning beds, but it was on the way to a perfect one. Something caught my eye while I was briefly standing to scan the lake in front of us. At first, I thought it was a mirage, a reflection of the glare on the lake surface that produced an image of a spawning circle. I took two paddle strokes and changed my angle of sight. It did not go away.

"Micah, do you see anything up ahead?"

"Like what?"

"I don't know. Anything?" I sat down and Micah stood up.

"Yes. Over there," he said, pointing. He sat down and I started paddling toward the place where he'd pointed. Micah stood up again.

"What is that?" he said, with more intensity than was typical of Micah's laid-back manner.

"What?" I asked.

"That!" he said, this time pointing much closer to the canoe and looking down. I stopped paddling, stood, and saw it too.

"What the—?" Now we both stood, a definite no-no for which we'd be forgiven this one time. There, on the bottom, in four to five feet of water, was an enormous white ring, several times the diameter of a hula hoop. It was a perfect circle with raised, white edges and a seemingly bottomless black hole in its center. We floated right over it, neither one of us speaking.

All around the shape, outside of its white edge, was the dark, muddy bottom, but the raised edge of the disc was light-colored sand, meaning that, under the mud, there must have been sand. We couldn't see to the bottom of the hole in the center, nor was I carrying an anchor to test the depth. An eerie feeling struck both of us at the same time. Micah looked at me for an explanation. I had none. I'd never seen anything remotely like this. Floating there in silence, we both forgot all about fishing. We kept drifting over and back again, trying to come up with an idea of what this was.

"It looks like a volcano," Micah said. Micah knew what one would look like. He'd been back to his native country several times since his adoption, a country that had sixteen active volcanoes.

"Which would mean an eruption from under the lake," I ventured. I remembered a friend of mine, a limnologist from Upstate New York. His passion for the study of all aspects of lakes, including their anaerobic layers and what lay beneath, was never more fervent than when a lake in Central Africa blew up in 1986. I remembered the news stories and the pictures myself. Thousands of dead cows and other livestock were strewn throughout the valley in Cameroon where Lake Nyos was located. Nearly 1800 people were killed, many of them in their sleep. My friend immediately traveled to the area with a team of geologists and a camera crew from *National Geographic*. What they found was death and destruction all around the lake. "Lymnic eruption" was the name given to the catastrophic event, virtually unknown before this time. Theories were proffered by scientists on what had led to the disaster, none of them definitive: a movement of tectonic plates, a landslide, an undetected earthquake, or a small volcanic eruption below the bed of the lake. That was the theory that came home to me now, as I stared down at the giant disc under my canoe.

The outcome in Cameroon was carbon dioxide gas that the lake spewed up, forming a toxic cloud that then moved through the valley, killing cattle and humans alike. It was odorless, there was no warning, and it happened while most people slept. The lake was not big. In fact, it was almost exactly the same size as the body of water we were now on—390 acres, about a mile and a half long. An eruption like the one alluded to in the mini-volcano theory would surely cause a crater. Possibly a crater just like the one we were looking at.

Micah had earned his college degree in cybertechnology from Roger Williams University in Providence, so he had the kind of inquisitive mind that would be triggered by something like this. "What about something from above?"

I looked below us again, and of course, he was right. An object plunging into the lake from the sky would also form a crater. With great force, it would have shot down through the lake bed, displacing material on the bottom to form a disc with raised edges, just like this. A meteor? We were in a very remote area, miles from anything resembling civilization. The skies over the West Grand Lake system and the St. Croix Valley are busy with meteor showers every summer. A stray fire burst going into this arm at the northern reaches of the system would likely go unnoticed.

Likewise, had a mini volcano erupted beneath this lake, it might have easily escaped observation, even if there were some moose or deer lying dead in the woods from carbon dioxide poisoning.

Fishing fell by the wayside for the remainder of that morning. Micah and I floated in circles, thoughts drifting through all kinds of possibilities, never really settling on one over another. Later I would read that craters are sometimes formed on the bottoms of lakes where water levels are manipulated drastically, after being completely drained and refilled, for example, but that wouldn't apply here. Besides, the craters formed in those instances were a fraction of the size of this one.

When we arrived at the lunch ground to meet the rest of the party with just one pickerel, everyone knew something was up. Of course, the punch that our discovery packed was lost in the translation. The lunch ground was a long way from our sighting, and no one wanted to lose fishing time to go find it. That was all right. Like other mysteries I'd encountered, this one would be best kept between those of us who had experienced it, adding another dimension to the bond Micah and I already had.

I went back maybe four times that summer, always alone. Each time the outer rim of the crater was darker than the last, due to silting in. The hole remained, but the disc became less discernible. This meant that, when Micah and I made our discovery, the event that had caused it had just happened. If anyone saw it, they said nothing. In towns this size, it takes less than that to make a headline. If it had become news, it wouldn't have caused the uproar that it might someplace else. Another unexplained phenomenon? One can almost get used to them around here.

12

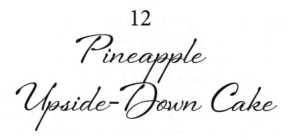

Pineapple
Upside-Down Cake

It had been very nearly an open winter, and now it was a late spring, with enough snow and cold to make up for the mild season that had come before. I'd wanted to make this trip sooner, but weather, mud, and late snowstorms had stalled it until Memorial Day.

Finally, the trail was open, exposing matted leaves and the deep hoof impressions of moose and deer that had availed themselves of the easy walking. We tend to think that these large game animals prefer walking in thickets, where they're less likely to be seen. But brush out a trail through those thickets and see what happens. You'll have yourself a game highway.

There was still some snow in the dark woods, under hemlock trees and at the base of big boulders. Several robins flushed up from the trail in front of me, and I was happy to see them. Cold had been this spring's main feature. In fact, this had been the trend in recent years: a protracted spring that felt like an extension of winter, followed by an extended summer, leading into fall weather that lasted to Christmas.

These changes were being welcomed by some and denied by others, but at the other end of the trail I was walking lived someone who'd begun recognizing them many years before they ever made the news. It would certainly come up in our conversation later today.

From years of hiking out here, I've accumulated certain waypoints that help me gauge how far I've come and how far I have to go. The first one is a rock with spruce tree roots encircling it. I've always marveled at the way a tree will incorporate a rock, or even another tree, as it grows. Sometimes, massive roots grow large enough to move rocks. They have bark on them, just like the main body of the tree—they are, after all, exposed, like the rest of the tree. In this case, one of these exposed roots made the perfect backrest, wrapped around a rounded rock perfectly positioned for my first rest along the trail.

I set down my pack basket and pulled out my thermos of coffee. With the temperature flirting with forty when I left the house, I was dressed in fewer layers than usual, making it easy to walk under the sweat threshold. Just as I sat down, I heard something in the woods, well off of the trail. When I looked in the direction of the sound, I saw a black shape moving away from me fast. That's what a black bear does when the scent of a human reaches its nostrils.

I wasn't surprised. The previous week, I'd lost a bird feeder to a bear raid for the third year in a row. I wondered how many more it would take before I smartened up. For the bears to be already in circulation seemed out of rhythm to me. It was still cold, there was nothing to eat, and yet out of the dens they came, on the prowl for anything, including black oil sunflower seeds. I always find these massacred bird feeders in the woods, about two hundred yards away from where the thief stole them. The plexiglass is always perforated with holes from the bear's sharp teeth, and it's usually broken in half besides. This is running into money.

As the black shape slipped out of sight into thicker woods, I thought of Alonzo Bacon. Could I have confused what I'd just seen if I'd been in the shoes of the hunter that mistook Alonzo for a bear? I guessed it was possible, but it would seem you'd have to shoot fast, before truly verifying the target. Too late is too bad in hunting; you very often get only one opportunity to bag a big game animal. It comes unexpectedly and is gone just as fast. I don't know how hungry those men were. I was pretty certain that what I'd just seen was a bear. Nothing else out here running in these woods is that black and that big. I would've had only a split second to shoot, but what if I was wrong?

I'd had my fill of coffee by the time I scared myself with this train of thought. Now I'd be hiking a good forty-five minutes before my next break at a stream that runs full and fast at this time of year. I'd barely stopped thinking of the man who shot Alonzo Bacon and found my woods-walking rhythm again when I was startled by a woodcock that flushed six feet in front of me. Well, I laughed to myself, I was in the perfect mood to be startled. The whistling flight and zig-zag flight pattern were the unmistakable signs that timberdoodles were returning. A month to six weeks from now, they'd be on their singing grounds, swept up in their amazing mating ritual.

The day warmed. The first purple finches I'd seen showed up on a beech tree limb. Memorial Day was late for them to be making their first appearance. I'm only an amateur bird watcher, with a Sibley's in both bathrooms at home and one at camp, but there's always so much mystery left over, even after you've read up on your favorite species. Maybe that's what I love about it. Somewhere on this walk, I knew I'd run into the same pair of pileated woodpeckers I almost always see on the way in. Last time I was in here, it was on snowshoes, and they had practically felled two eastern white pines along the trail. There were huge piles of chips and sawdust at the base of each tree. The holes they make are almost always rectangular in shape. It seems that's the most effective way to excavate what they're looking for: carpenter ants. These pests to people are banquet fare for this feathered connoisseur. Carpenter ants ball up inside trees in winter like a sticky mass of sap, but it's a nutrition gold strike for pileateds. Trouble is, once they make these large holes, other birds are attracted to them to feed and even nest in them. Still, this largest of woodpeckers has other problems. It surprised me to find out how many predators they have. A goshawk will take a mature pileated down— no small feat for them, but this is probably light work for a great horned owl, another of its predators. Bobcats and pine martens can sneak up on them before they can take wing. Snakes, weasels, and squirrels will raid their nests for eggs in April. Why, I wondered, don't they just turn that fifteen-beats-per-second cordless beak loose on these predators and drill them into Swiss cheese? If you've ever heard the sound of that pecking in the echo chamber of a hardwood forest, your first thought was most likely a jackhammer.

I could hear the stream before I came to it—that sound used by massage therapists to put patients into a dreamy calm. Where the trail crosses it, there's a dead water stretching thirty yards upstream and twenty yards downstream. I looked out over it from the cedar log bridge that has been there since the first time I found myself out here, fifteen years earlier. It's a little worse for wear now, but still serviceable. I looked up and down the edges of the stream for cutaways in the bank. I had no trouble finding them. They look like erosion, like the current is carving out the edges to make the stream wider. Then I saw what I was really looking for: a vertical rod sticking up out of the water next to one of these cutaways. A few feet away, there was another. I knew that, if I walked up to each one of these rods, right below the surface, secured to the rod, there would be a steel coil trap with a round pan in the center where a muskrat would step, releasing the springs. Muskrats are the cause of the cutaways. They eat the roots of plant life growing at the stream's edges. The roots hold the bank intact. When they're gone, the rest erodes. The dens of muskrats are up under the bank, so my friend had put his sets in strategic locations. I didn't want to disturb them, but I got close enough to see a still-uneaten carrot suspended above both pans. He has long told me that there's no better bait for a muskrat than a carrot.

I took off my pack basket, found a seat on a log, and let the smile I felt in my chest radiate. The fact that there were fresh traps here meant that my friend was all right. It meant that three-quarters of my mission out here was already fulfilled. If I wasn't mistaken, my friend would turn ninety on his next birthday. For the past two years, I'd been coming out to Township Unknown twice each season instead of once, as before. He'd noticed it too but hadn't complained. In fact, when I unpacked that huge bag of carrots when I'd snowshoed out here in January, I thought his face might crack from the smile that creased it from one side to the other.

Muskrats are very important in Drummond Humchuck's life. They are food, income, bait, exercise, and activity. Previously, he had shown me how he skins a muskrat by suspending it by its tail, snipping off its front claws, making incisions down the inside of each back leg, then simply undressing it of its plush coat. It is then ready to dry on a stretcher, either for sale or for his own uses. Once the skin is off, you can turn the muskrat onto its back and see the castors, or scent glands, at the top of each hind leg. Their soft, gelatinous substance might remind you of fish roe sacks, though castors are much more powerful in odor. It is not uncommon for a quart of these (half a dozen to ten muskrats) to fetch seventy-five to a hundred dollars. They're in demand as bait, for scent, and for various exotic purposes in other parts of the world. Drummond, with no bank account, investments, or financial nest egg, has no use for the money itself. It's just the supplies it can be traded for that have any value to him, and that's where his Native friend Mihku and I come in.

It was now late morning. My two-and-a-half-hour hike was three-quarters done, and it has always been on this last leg of the journey that I reflect on my discovery of Township Unknown fifteen years earlier. There should have been little or no chance of Drummond Humchuck and me ever meeting. He lives farther away from me than many guiding clients of mine from neighboring states. But certain fortuitous things can only happen to you when you're lost, as I learned on the day I met Drummond. I go over this every time I'm out here looking at the old hash marks I made on trees along the trail on my way out that first time. I had stumbled onto this trail while tracking a large buck who'd shown himself to me just once, back in country I could still recognize. Tracking can get you into trouble. You are so engrossed, so smitten from having seen him, that you can be separated from reason. What you're hoping for is that moment that so often happens with deep woods bucks. They become exasperated with whatever it is that's following them, much like Butch Cassidy and the Sundance Kid atop the mesa, looking down across the valley at the dust rising from the obstinate riders on their trail for days. "Who are those guys?" Butch says. "They're starting to get on my nerves." At some point, the buck feels the same, so he stops and waits. Holds his ground. Gets a look to satisfy his curiosity. Which means you get a look too, and maybe a shot.

It never happened. Once I reached this very stream where I now sat, the buck track disappeared, which meant that my quarry had walked in the stream. But which way? Up or down? I'd wandered so far from my home hunting grounds that I had no landmark for where I was—a problem that didn't matter to me as long as I could still see the tracks. But, during my hours-long chase, the temperature had come up enough to melt the covering of snow. Then I saw the cedar bridge across the stream. Someone had to have put it there, I reasoned, and therefore, maybe this trail led to something. I followed it, feeling a little embarrassed. No seasoned hunter or guide ever admits to being lost. We simply get "turned around."

The trail led to something alright, and I have that elusive buck to thank. Literature is rich with these references: revenants that appear to people as majestic stags. It is a concept baked into fairy tales read to children over centuries. Also, experienced hunters will tell stories of tracks in the snow that came, to their utter frustration, to a complete and unequivocal end. Period. They'd walk in wider and wider circles on the assumption that the great animal, with its legendary leaping ability, had made a

154

long jump in one direction or another—only to be left with the vexing conclusion that the beast they'd been tracking had simply atomized. Anyone who has experienced this can attest that it's a very hard pill to swallow. We'd all rather believe in human error, that we got something wrong, messed up somewhere, than believe that we were being led by what we were chasing, into the mystic.

These are the reflections that get me down the final leg. These days, I'm no longer lost in Township Unknown. Wasn't it written someplace that, wherever a true friend resides, you have a home? After our first meeting, I was wondering how long this odd friendship of ours could last. Drummond was already an older man, even then. My concern quickly subsided when I realized his uncanny skills. If I had to learn how to make a pair of mittens out of muskrat, using sinew for thread and fish bones for needles, it would surely take months or years to perfect. He'd actually been doing that when we first met in his cabin doorway, and I'd wondered if I'd stumbled onto some kind of Rip Van Winkle. I soon saw my error. In that Washington Irving tale, Rip had fled to the forest to escape work. Drummond was no Rip Van Winkle. He was at work constantly, even if he didn't call it that.

"The old ways" are nothing most of us are interested in revisiting. But to Drummond, these aren't "old ways" at all, but are instead his means of getting by reasonably well. This takes many skills and no small degree of ingenuity. We would no doubt mourn being cast into a predicament where we had to put such skills to use. We rely on others to make almost everything we need, do most of what we don't want to do, and amuse us out of an immutable boredom. Imagine the antithesis: a life in which you are never bored, because before that ever has a chance to happen, you're already on to the next task. Meet my friend, Drummond Humchuck.

His boots are laced with cedar sinew, an incredibly strong and resilient material. Once they're spent, it's easy enough to remove a swatch of bark from a live cedar tree (which grow in abundance around his cabin) and then take the still-moist strips from inside the bark. There are myriad uses for these stringy, leathery strips in all kinds of repairs. If you're giving your cabin slippers a new life with the raw material you've harvested from a tree growing outside your house, can you really say you're bored while you're doing that? Or that your life lacks meaning? If you're able to cure leather items of your own making with bear grease you've made from rendered bear fat from a bear you killed, where exactly does boredom fit into this scheme? If a very agreeable sustenance results from harvesting the local, indigenous mast crop of nuts and berries, as well as your own domestic root crops, and then supplementing this with hunting, trapping, and fishing, is "predicament" the right term for this way of life?

The more likely predicament would be loneliness, but loneliness hitches a ride on the backs of inactivity and silence. We've already addressed inactivity. In other writings, I've given accounts of how Drummond pierces the quiet of his hideaway with an extravagance uncommon in the world at large, never mind in the wilds of Maine. He is a "siffleur," which is a rare word, and rightly so, since it applies to a rare person—the symphonic whistler. I've told of hearing these concerts from far down the trail as the notes reverberate through vast tracts of wilderness. His repertoire resides in the vault of his memory. When something awakens a specific memory, a composition comes out of Drummond that I never knew was there, and just possibly, he didn't either.

Another word on silence… To say that the environs of Township Unknown, where Drummond Humchuck's cabin is located, are silent would be to admit to not having spent much time in a forest. Silent? Anything but. When I stop walking and sit for ten minutes several times on my way in, I find it impossible to pick out every single sound as separate. Besides the trills, chirps, and warbles, besides the calling and the pecking and the pounding of a partridge drumming, besides the muted howl of the wind high in the hemlocks, there is a chatter that suffuses every other sound. It may come from crickets, peep frogs, plus a host of other creatures, the sum of whose emanations forms a cacophony. You can wish it would stop if you're still-hunting from a stump or a deer stand, waiting to hear the footfall of a buck deer approaching. In all likelihood, the buck uses those sounds to aid him in his stealth. In summary, the woods are talking all the time.

To Drummond, who has been listening to the cacophony of the forest most of his life without interference from electronics, it is better described as a language. Admittedly, it has taken me a long time to understand this—how he can hear alerts and other messages in what is surely a foreign tongue to most of us. All of my visits are unannounced, just as with Mihku, Drummond's eeling partner, who comes out here on a different route from Indian Township. He knows we're both coming eventually, but neither of us can get word to him, so he can't know exactly when. For years, the thing that baffled me to no end was that he was always expecting me when I arrived. There were times I became so frustrated by this sixth sense of his that I took to mischief. I'd purposely interrupt the rhythm of my visits and show up when I wasn't supposed to. He has never been surprised by my appearance. There has always been a fresh pot of tea ready on his wood cookstove, and from his demeanor, it has always been obvious that he knew I was coming. The answer, the explanation, is this vocabulary, spoken by the living forest, that he is attuned to. It embarrasses me, as a Maine guide who conducts all of his business outdoors, that I can't translate this language into intelligible messages the way he does. I've watched the way he listens during our periods of quiet together. It is unencumbered by any busyness or clutter in his mind. For me, things can get in the way of this kind of listening—schedules, worries, deadlines.

Drummond, however, is an open channel, able to pick up the signals and messages that his environment is communicating.

Because of its mistaken omission from efforts to map millions of wild acres into thirty-six-square-mile townships, Township Unknown is a unique place. Its brilliant disguise—hiding in plain sight amidst a sea of anonymous townships with numbers for names—has enabled it to escape all the things that they haven't: roads, logging, traffic, snoopers. Not having been mapped, it is only found the way I found it, by being lost. Because of its unique circumstances in escaping "progress," it is more boreal, more primeval than the woods most of us usually walk in. It may be that its language is purer because of this. That's my own speculation. But that it speaks, and that Drummond hears and understands, is no speculation at all.

Having seen my friend's active "rat traps" in the stream, I struck a lively pace the last leg of my journey. On that leg, I remembered a piece of mail that had come to my home just the day before. It was the form from the U.S. Census Bureau. The thought brought a smile. Drummond Humchuck, sole resident of Township Unknown, has surely never been counted. In fact, this year the Bureau was offering twenty dollars per hour for temps who were willing to go to households and conduct the official survey. There were only two people on earth that I know of who could conceivably count Drummond in the U.S. Census. Those two are Mihku and me. Therefore, he will continue to go uncounted, and therefore not to exist, this being his principal means of ensuring privacy and protecting his way of life.

The clearing where Drummond's cabin stands is the only open area in all that country, except for where streams widen into ponds, opening up the skyline overhead. When Drummond and Mihku's father built this cabin in the 1950s, they cleared enough trees to allow five to six hours of sunlight to reach the ground where Drummond would grow his root crops. The arc of the sun is high enough from May to September to afford him a substantial larder of potatoes, rutabaga, carrots, onions, and parsnips. He harvests his parsnips right after the frost goes out of the ground in spring. "Nevah sweetah," he's told me many times.

When I stepped into the clearing, I received a slight scare. Not to find my friend sitting in his doorway expecting me was abnormal. But just then, a voice boomed out of the shed beside the cabin: "Any rats in them traps, chum?"

I blew out a big sigh of relief. "Not yet," I called back. "Looks like you just set 'em this morning."

"Yep. Been comin' good, though." That was the long and short of my welcome, but it was typical of our salutations. Drummond always speaks to me as if I hadn't really left after my last visit. "Maybe after tea you can give me a hand."

Inside the shed, stretcher boards were lined up on his bench, next to a pile of dead muskrats. I knew now what he had in store for me, and that he'd timed this task for my arrival. As I got closer, I did as I always do: took a full measure of him to see what changes, if any, were detectible. This is a subtle science, since I don't want him to notice. Over the years, he has adjusted himself to physical changes, and compensated so that they don't really limit him the way they might someone else. If a heel is ailing him, he applies bag balm or one of his other remedies to it, puts extra padding in his boot, and carries on, even if he has to favor the sore foot. If he has sustained an abrasion from one of his many activities, he uses bogwani, the poplar-based oil, essentially benzine, that he makes himself seasonally for cuts and burns.

Anyone might reasonably ask, "But hasn't he slowed down?" The answer is yes, of course, the way most highly active people slow down—almost imperceptibly. If you were walking down the trail behind him, you wouldn't be able to guess his age. I sometimes note new hitches in his gait or added arm movements to provide propulsion, all of which keep his forward progress pretty much the same. What he does now that he never used to do is insert sit-down breaks more often during the day. They must be restorative, because when he's had his tea, or his brief "peek behind the eyelids," as he calls it, he picks up the task at hand at the same pace as before. I wonder at these adjustments, thinking maybe I could learn from him how to slow the inexorable onslaught of age. It may also help that he is not constantly comparing himself to others of his own vintage. The only two people he sees are both decades younger than him. If elderly people surrounded only by other elderly people seem to "act their age," then it may follow that they will do the same in the company of their juniors.

Once the tea is poured—black alder tea to "loosen the tongue," as Drummond says—we have our traditional Christmas moment. That's when I unload the pack basket of supplies I've brought him. If you can remember the way you felt as a child when you saw presents under the tree on Christmas morning, the look on Drummond's face as I unload the contents captures that moment. "Ooooh," he'll sigh when he sees something he's recently run out of, or is about to. I try to correspond my selections with his seasonal activities. When he saw a big box of pushpin-type tacks come out of the basket, he was more than relieved. "We'll need them today!" he effused. Once the muskrats were "skun" and fleshed out, they'd be pulled down over a basswood stretcher board, fur side down. The leathery tail gets snipped off at this point, but then the edges of the hide want to curl up. Pushpins keep them in place. Once it is cured, he can take the tacks out, and the whole thing retains its shape. How much each fur will fetch depends on its size and condition. Drummond already knows the size. There are marks on the basswood board that indicate small, medium, large, and extra-large. Whichever marker the hide comes to when it is fully pulled down over the board, that's its size. He takes great care that every one of his catches is in pristine condition. These critters aren't shot, after all, and so there are no holes other than nostrils, ears, and eyes.

The next thing my friend ogled at was an assortment of things not normally included in the wangan I bring. He watched silently and inquisitively as I pulled out a can of Dole pineapples, a box of yellow cake mix, a jar of Maraschino cherries, an egg rolled up in a sock, a plastic bag with brown sugar in it, and a new roll of aluminum foil. Drummond looked at this loot for a long moment, then eyeballed me.

"Pineapple upside-down cake?" he asked, with a childish twinkle in his eye. I had an idea he'd remember this dessert, which would've been much more common in his day than now.

"You bet," I replied. "Still got that Dutch oven?"

"Yessah!" I knew I'd seen one in his shed, and I sure didn't want to lug one out here on my back.

"Let's do it after we work," I offered. So far, this was a typical visit, beginning with my feeble attempt to surprise him, which always fails. Then my discovery of the chore we're going to do together, which he has staged and readied for my arrival. Then our tea and talk. I sometimes hear a story during this period that takes me down a few more fathoms into my friend's past—his life before Township Unknown. I've learned I can never urge or beckon this out of him. It must come of its own accord, when something sparks a memory from bygone years, and then it spills out like the basket of cranberries I bring him in the fall.

The last thing to come out of today's basket was a gross of popsicle sticks, which always earns the biggest "ooooooh" of all. He surely knew, or at least hoped, that they were coming, as I'd already unpacked the glue and a passel of toothpicks that he uses for some of the finer work involved in his models. I've described some of these elaborate works elsewhere, the last completed masterwork being the Titanic. This has special meaning for him because of an aunt whose honeymoon, a passage from New York to London, was booked on the return trip of the ill-fated ship—a trip that never happened. I'd noticed the minute I'd entered the cabin that there was a large work in progress on the table he uses for model-making.

"Can you give me a hint?" I asked, nodding toward it.

"New Yawk Public Library," he answered, almost as though it should be obvious. The edifice had already taken shape, including the great arched doors and windows. I wondered how in the world he was going to handle the two lions, Patience and Fortitude, that watch over the entrance from either side. The greater question, however, was what he was working from, other than memory. There was no open book near the model, no poster or picture to go by.

"More tea?" he asked, probably sensing my well of questions. I took the last sip of the black alder tea and set down my cup.

"No thanks, Drum. How about we make short work of those muskrats so I can bake you a cake?" A sudden change of expression came over Drummond's face. Before I could decide whether to be alarmed by this, a broad smile spread his beard out. Then, he leaned back in his seat, formed an odd shape with his mouth, and blew out the first whole stanza of "If I Knew You Were Comin' I'd've Baked a Cake," a song, I later learned, that was a chart-topper at the same time as the cake I was going to make was at its peak of popularity. Such were the endearing surprises that were commonplace in the company of Township Unknown's woods wizard. "Yessah!" he smiled, leading the way out the cabin door. This is what often happened when something that came up spontaneously linked him directly to a fond memory, in this case, one he could whistle.

Between the cabin and the shed is the outdoor fireplace where, in the past, we have heated and rendered bear fat, made lye soap, and cooked a mess of late summer white perch, among other things. Lying beside the rocks were several strips of birch bark and a pile of cedar kindling. "You mind?" I asked, pulling a lighter from my pocket. "Have at 'er," Drummond smiled. Other than distillates, there is no faster fire than birch bark and dry cedar. It was roaring in fifteen seconds. I added a few small split beech chunks to the fireplace and left it.

Inside the shed, beside the stack of dead muskrats on the bench, was a bowl, already half full of castors. The musk emitted from it was far from *eau de toilette*. I hoped that, after working over it for a while, I'd get used to it. Deft as a magician, I watched

Drummond skin the first rat in under a minute. He handed me a fleshing tool, along with the hide, and said, "Firm but gentle." I'd watched him enough times that I knew what he meant. When the hide, which was still in one piece after he "undressed" the rat, was turned inside out, there were fat deposits that clung to the skin. With firm strokes delivered at an angle, the fleshing tool will remove it. Later, we'd use the same type of stroke to brush out the fur with a bristle brush. Drummond's final step before moving on to skin the next muskrat in the pile was to flip the denuded muskrat carcass, stomach up, and remove the two castors, one from the top of each thigh.

The skins accumulated beside me as I struggled to keep up. Finally, Drummond stopped and looked at me with his trademark ironic grin. "Little quicker if you can stand it, chum," he said, and laughter exploded out of me. I did get the hang of it after eight or ten skins, and then the work went fast. The basswood stretchers looked a little like paddle blades sawed off in the middle and then made narrower at the tip. The skins stretched easily over them, with Drummond stretching and me tacking. At the base of each board was a hole so that it could hang on a nail for the next day or two.

"Good batch," I said, admiring the large bowl now full of rat glands. I'd also noticed that the majority of skins fell between the large and extra-large markings on the boards.

"Yep," Drummond agreed. "Mihku'll pick up them glands next trip." With both Mihku and me having doubled our seasonal trips, it was now rare that Drummond went a month without seeing one of us.

Before leaving the shed, I took down the Dutch oven from its perch on a big spike in one of the timbers. Its weight took me by surprise. It had three "feet" welded onto the bottom so that the oven could sit above the coals. The lid was concave so that it could hold more coals, providing heat from the top too—thus the oven effect.

There are birch twig chairs all over Drummond's property so that, no matter what activity he's involved in, he can always take a load off and get a peek behind his eyelids. Drummond has built these chairs so that the center of gravity is calibrated precisely to his body. They are not, strictly speaking, straight-back chairs, but instead recline slightly so that, when he nods off, his head doesn't fall forward. The whole episode lasts no longer than twenty minutes, after which time he opens his eyes but doesn't move for several minutes more. Then he comes alive again, fully refreshed and ready to return to his busy life.

Not today. Today he could relax and luxuriate in one of man's most cherished pastimes: watching someone else work. I poured it on, knowing that, for him, this show would be the equivalent of the Cirque du Soleil. I'd brought out the things I needed for the Dutch oven while Drummond set a new pot of tea on the wood cookstove inside. After he took his seat, I peeled off two large sections of aluminum foil from the roll and laid them over the open cast-iron pot. Then, using my hands, I pressed down, shaping the foil to the contour of the oven, careful to give myself a smooth, flat bottom. I then pressed the foil against the sides before putting the lid back on securely. I trimmed off the excess foil that hung out from under the lid, then picked up the Tupperware bowl I'd brought along for mixing. Into it I emptied the yellow cake mix. At this, Drummond retrieved his red willow pouch from his shirt pocket, then filled and lit his pipe with a wooden match. He was giving his full concentration to the spectacle unfolding in front of him.

Rather than ask my friend what he was using these days to open cans, I took out my Swiss Army knife and went around the rim of the Dole pineapple can with the opener blade. "Save that lid, chum!" Drummond piped when it came loose in my hand. I didn't have to ask why. I'd already seen what he uses lids for: when a hole appears in the cabin floor from wear and tear or mice or a gnawing porcupine underneath, he patches it with a tin can lid and roofing nails. The floor was pock-marked with them. Holding the pineapples back with my thumb, I poured all of the juice into the bowl with the cake mix. To this I added the egg that had made the trip to Township Unknown safely rolled up in a sock. As I had no wire whisk, I used a whittled hookaroon (the hooked sapling stick used by guides cooking shore lunches) to mix the ingredients. I made sure to let Drummond see everything up close, in case he wanted to repeat this at a later date. My batter was a little too thick. Shelley had prepared me for this. If I found that to be the case even after the juice and the egg, she said, "Add a little bit of this," handing me a can of ginger ale. "The carbonation will make the cake fluffier." Drummond could see that the batter was dense, but his face lit up when he saw the ace I had in the bottom of the pack basket. When I'd added about a quarter cup of ginger ale to the mix, I gave him the rest. Watching him react to the ginger ale fizz on his tongue was like watching a child eat cotton candy.

Pronouncing the batter perfect, I got out the plastic bag with the third of a cup of brown sugar in it. This was sprinkled and smoothed out evenly on the bottom of the Dutch oven. It would form a glaze when the heat hit it. I was then able to fit seven pineapple slices in the bottom of the pot, and into the center of each one, I placed a Maraschino cherry. Drummond and I admired this face with seven eyes looking up at us, his eyes shining every bit as brightly, so much so that I thought for a moment they were tearing up. I made a few adjustments to the beech coals in the fire, which had by now settled, separating some out for the Dutch oven lid. Satisfied, I picked up my bowl and, using the hookaroon, helped every last bit of batter into the pot, spreading it evenly over the pineapples and cherries. After placing the lid onto the oven, I hooked the oven's bale with my stick and lifted it onto the circle of coals I'd made in the fire pit. Beech is an excellent wood for cooking, and its coals last longer than those of many other hardwoods. Not having tongs or fire gloves, I used two pieces of Drummond's cedar kindling as chopsticks to lift coals onto the oven lid. When I was satisfied, having spread them around for an even heat, I glanced over to Drummond to see if he approved as well. I looked once, then looked back. The whiskers on his chin were twitching. Then I saw that his chin was trembling.

"What is it, Drum?"

He did the best he could to collect himself by tamping down the red willow in his pipe and puffing it alive again. "Oh, I seen this once before, is all."

Now that my dessert was set to bake, I took a seat in another twig chair opposite him and leaned forward.

"Seen what, Drum?"

"This right heeah," he replied, pointing his pipe toward the fire.

"Pineapple-upside down cake?"

"Yep. But they done it in spidahs." I knew that in the early days of its popularity, pineapple upside-down cake was often made in a cast-iron frying pan (sometimes called a "spider"), or even in a cake tin. All you needed was a lid. But it certainly wasn't this that had set my friend's whiskers into a quiver. I recognized now that the moment had changed. This didn't happen often, but when it did, Drummond's face altered. With his thousand-yard stare, he was seeing something I couldn't see, something from another time. I knew better than to do anything but wait. Wait to see if he wanted to bring this thing, whatever it was, out into the light of day.

"Lots of 'em," he said, still staring off into the distance.

"Cakes?"

"Hundreds. 'Magine?"

I waited for at least another three minutes, which is a very, very long time when you're waiting for someone to go on with their story, or, in this case, hoping that they will. Finally, after several puffs of red willow became gossamer halos above his head, Drummond said, "Creeah," then went silent again. I could tell that this word, whatever it meant, hadn't escaped his mouth for a very long time, as the mere act of saying it brought a wince across his face. For fifteen years I'd been making my trips out here, but there had always been an unspoken boundary between us, something I was made aware of without being told. I knew not to cross it, and by keeping to this practice, I was, on rare occasions, gifted with glimpses into the Drummond of long ago. That's how I learned about Mihku, and Moses, Mihku's father, who was Drummond's teacher, mentor, and best friend. He'd helped Drummond build his cabin, and they'd hunted, fished, and trapped together until Moses's untimely drowning while tending their eel sluice. Since Moses and Mihku were Passamaquoddy, I'd always speculated that my friend may have been raised in the tribe and might even have a Native bloodline.

Drummond looked up to the treetops, perhaps unsure if he wanted to go on. I looked up too, but I couldn't see what he was seeing, only that the buds of the red maples were plump. After a few more warm, sunny days, they'd open into tiny leaflets. Then it suddenly occurred to me that, in my friend's backwoods Maine dialect, he'd given me his pronunciation of "Korea," I decided to chance a slight nudge.

"You were in the war, Drum?" When he looked at me, I felt contrite, worried that I'd committed a transgression.

"Conflict," he corrected me. "They never called it a war."

"Yes," I agreed.

"But it were." I nodded again, rapidly juggling dates in my mind, struggling with my history and the chronology of events.

"The '50s?" I risked. Once again, his glance came down from the treetops to meet mine.

"Thanksgiving, 1950," he almost whispered, then he chuckled. "They flew in turkeys."

"They served you turkey? You had a Thanksgiving there—in Korea?"

"That's what we called it. Last hot meal for more 'n two weeks, 'cept it weren't hot." Drummond chuckled again. "Time you got it off yer tin plate, it was half froze. Good though." Here was a wider lens into my friend's life before Township Unknown than

I'd ever been given. I wanted to go slow, to honor it, but at the same time I feared he might not go on. Still mentally scanning dates, I realized that, since Drummond was about to turn ninety, he would've been twenty in 1950.

"You were in the army, Drum?"

"Yep. Eighth. Buck private."

"Where was this Thanksgiving?" It felt as if we'd passed a barrier between Drummond and these memories. He was in them now, seeing them. His eyes were focused far away from his cabin dooryard.

"Hagaru-ri," he answered, having no trouble getting his tongue around this tongue twister. "Chosin Reservoir." When he said this, he didn't say "chosen," giving the "s" a "z" sound. It came out with a distinctive "s" as though there should be no mistaking it. "The mess cooks made this," he said, pointing his pipe at the Dutch oven, "and the mail trucks brought mail. Mine was cookies from Moses's missus. I stuffed 'em in my shirt to warm 'em up. Last mail we seen for weeks. Last most of us ever saw." My coals above and below Drummond's Dutch oven were half black and half white, doing their job well enough that, in a half hour to forty-five minutes, I'd remove the lid and jab my cake with a stick to see if any batter stuck. Drummond looked at the fireplace too, but his thoughts had flown. He'd come to a place I'd seen only once or twice before. The only thing to do was let it happen. With all his stops and starts, all his deep sighs and even a few tears, Drummond let the story flow out of him as if reading it, line by line, in those red maple treetops.

Drummond said there were about 3300 of them there, and that was just the army. The marines were headed to the other side of the Chosin, which was the west side. The plan had come down from "on high," as he put it, meaning Douglas MacArthur, who was running things from Tokyo. He'd told the troops they'd be "home by Christmas," and who were they to doubt General MacArthur?

Receiving marching orders was one thing, but no one had foreseen the cold that they encountered in November in the mountains surrounding the Chosin. Drummond said he felt more fortunate than many because "they was from the South and never knew cold like that." Coming from an even more northerly latitude than northern Korea, Drummond had surely known it, lived in it, and worked in it. But he said his heart broke for what he saw around him. When it reached twenty and thirty below zero and the wind never let up, men who fell asleep froze to death. The first casualties in his unit were frostbite, and that came before a shot was ever fired.

The terrain was difficult for making trenches, bunkers, or berms. "Tough diggin' " was how Drummond described it, but I was picturing a mountainous landscape in sub-zero winter with nothing but an E-tool, the short army-issue shovel used for this work. Whatever they could build up around them also served as a wind barrier, but this alone was not enough to keep them warm. And it was crowded—however small that space might be, all of the weaponry, ammunition, bedding, mess kits, canteens, and men had to fit in it. Still, Drummond said, for all that, men found jokes to tell and things to laugh about. For the longest time, everybody thought that, once they reached the Yalu River, Korea's boundary with China, MacArthur would be proven right and they'd turn around and march south.

Drummond smiled when he told of watching their air support. His task force in the Eighth Army was at such an altitude in those mountains that they were looking down at the pilots flying through on their missions. "Sometimes," he said, "you could look right into the cockpits and see 'em wavin."

For those first long days and longer nights, the war Drummond's outfit was fighting was the cold. Medics worked around the clock to save toes, feet, and fingers, trying to stave off gangrene and amputations. They were all equal under a withering, relentless winter, which, for a while, seemed a much greater threat than the nonexistent enemy MacArthur had promised. Then, one evening at dusk, everything changed.

Drummond noticed a deer running down the ridge in front of his unit. It was the time of day when deer did come out, but then there was another one. Then another. More and more of them came, and they were bolting, not just moving. Next to Drummond in his shallow pit was a fellow from Wisconsin. Drummond told him those deer were being driven by something behind them. The two of them passed the word along to be on high alert.

Just before dark, with enough ambient light for the troops to see and feel something even more chilling than the cold that owned them all, the first wave of Chinese soldiers came down the same ridge where Drummond had seen all those deer. Men, in the thousands. Before they were halfway down it, another wave followed them. Not even the deafening, massive barrage from Drummond's unit was enough to drown out the sound of bugles and shouting that accompanied the Chinese onslaught. Drummond told the treetops (and me) that he still hears those bugles from time to time. And the shouting. But even more often, he sees the faces of the first Chinese soldiers who overran his unit.

A third wave followed the second, only they carried no rifles. It was planned. As they ran through, they picked up weapons from the dead. Drummond's weapon was an M1. He'd requested it because it fired the same .30-06 round as his deer and moose rifle back home, so it felt familiar to him. And just like back home, when temperatures dipped far below zero, you had to clean the rifle of any excess grease and oil, which could freeze and cause the weapon to seize. He passed along this tip to any who would listen, especially the boys from the south. He said the other weapons, like the M2 carbine and Browning Automatic rifles, were always jamming in that cold.

I was watching the scenes Drummond was describing play across his face as he spoke all of it in a low whisper. I remembered that, right after meeting him that first time, fifteen years earlier, I had written, "He's never talked specifically of his early life, although I know he hasn't been in Township Unknown forever. I've had a peculiar feeling that this world had shown a young Drummond Humchuck, perhaps through its wars, things that forged the man I know now. It's only speculation."

Now it was no longer speculation. In his story, I was tracing the origins of the deep lines I'd always studied on my friend's face. Those lines were a map of memories he was reliving now, accidentally, because of a pineapple upside-down cake.

The date, Drummond said, had always stuck with him—November 27—because that was the beginning. By daylight, all the bugles, the screaming, and shouting went silent. It was as if this massive Chinese army had never been there, except for what it left behind. Bodies lay frozen like sculptures, arms and legs akimbo, some reaching up as if to be saved. Drummond said his unit lost at least a third of its men that first night, November 27. The wounds of some of the survivors were actually aided by the cold, because blood coagulated and froze before a soldier could bleed out. Those were the lucky ones, but that luck ran out for many of them when their positions were overrun by Chinese soldiers who killed the defenseless wounded.

With such "tough digging," as Drummond put it, and so many bodies strewn everywhere, the enemy corpses were gathered and stacked during the daytime to form protective berms. It was one small measure of defense available when it became obvious that they were vastly outnumbered and surrounded. How must it have felt to Drummond to speak of these horrors out loud? I was struck dumb.

Airstrikes during the day weren't much use. With dawn, after the night's attacks, tens of thousands of the Chinese People's Volunteer Army, as it was called, just vanished. It was assumed that they'd gone underground. But every night, for seventeen nights, they reappeared and attacked again, from all sides. Drummond emptied his weapon over and over, so rapidly that the barrel melted the ice on his gloves and the water seeped through and burned his hands. He had confidence in his aim, having grown up as a hunter, but many times, he saw his round hit home but not stop the enemy soldier, who kept coming, sometimes not succumbing until his body draped lifeless over Drummond's rifle rest. All of their positions were girdled by thousands of Chinese soldiers as soon as nightfall came. They had no idea that the situation was exactly the same for the marines on the west side of the Chosin. There may have been as many as 130,000 Chinese soldiers who had crossed the Yalu to deny MacArthur the easy victory he'd promised.

Drummond hadn't puffed his pipe for several minutes. It lay, clenched in his fist, in his lap, as he looked seventy years distant into a life he'd once lived, a life that was maybe better forgotten. I had no experience to help me understand such things. At the same time, he was speaking as if he too needed to hear it. As if something was being uncovered, something that had been buried too long.

He said that his commanding officer was killed and replaced, and that the replacement was killed too. Their positions had been whittled down to a pathetically small group of stragglers. They came to the decision to make their way south during daylight. It would be too dangerous to take the road they'd used from Hagaru-ri, so they slogged through deep snow and scaled cliffs to get to the other side of the mountain. At this point they turned south, paralleling the road. Even here, they lost more men to snipers. Drummond said that their dwindling ranks were a pitiful sight: some wounded, some frostbitten, some dragging the body of a buddy behind them. He stopped briefly after telling this part. I didn't know if it was because of the difficulty of what he'd already told, or because he was anticipating what followed.

Those foundering few knew they had miraculously escaped insurmountable odds. Shouldn't they be dead too? Why weren't they? Then came the hallucination that they were, in fact, dead. All fear was gone now. What replaced it was a kind of anesthetic consciousness in which a man dutifully obeyed the mandate of survival. The ragtag group barely spoke to one another. Everyone had lost their friends; everyone had witnessed the same horrors. All that was left was this bewildering will to live that they were all harnessed to. A bedraggled, frozen few slogged on, most of them strangers and yet brothers to each other, in a hell they wouldn't have believed existed.

Each time he felt life and death flipping a coin over his fate, Drummond found himself turning to what he knew. It was his training from the elders of the tribe who'd taken him out many times into similar weather conditions. By the time he was thirteen, he'd slept under canoes during blizzards. He'd built lean-tos for overnights while tracking game in winter. His skills for making fast fires were unmatched by anyone in his Eighth Army unit. Whenever they found relative shelter in caves or rock outcroppings, Drummond knew how to produce fire from what looked like nothing. He knew that even the scat of wild animals would burn under some conditions, and so would some green wood or the bark of certain trees. His ragtag group kept these thawing respites brief to avoid signaling the enemy with smoke.

At the mention of smoke, I remembered my dessert and jumped up. Not wanting to interrupt or cause my friend to lose the thread, I made it quick, lifting the lid for a peak. We were still in good shape. If Drummond had noticed my movement, he didn't let on.

At times, something resembling a smile almost formed on his face. One of these moments was when he told me about feeling something chafing against the skin of his lower back as they trudged along the mountain passes on snow and ice. Some of the men had untreated wounds that they'd never felt because of numbness from the cold. All of them were spattered with dried, frozen blood, either from themselves, from someone they'd fought beside, or from Chinese soldiers. With the chafing he was feeling, Drummond wondered if he might've been grazed by a round after all. If so, he didn't care to see it, but finally the discomfort brought him to the point of reaching through all of his layers until he felt under his shirt in the back. Instead of blood on his hand, he came up with two cookies from the box he'd opened at Hagaru-ri on Thanksgiving. The smile that almost stretched across my friend's face gave way to tears that leaked out of the corners of his eyes and disappeared into the deep lines of his cheeks. He said he shared the cookies with someone walking beside him, someone he didn't know and never saw again.

"Funny, though… I can still see his face when I handed him that cookie." Right now, that face was perched somewhere among the maple buds, high overhead. I didn't need to see it. I was looking at one just like it, right in front of me.

A Dutch oven dessert had triggered all this, way out here in Township Unknown, where Drummond had been relatively safe from triggers for most of his life. Maybe he hadn't known whether he'd be able to let all of this out. I think we were both surprised; him at doing it, and me at being trusted enough to hear it.

I was about to stand up and prepare a spot on the stump Drummond and I used as an outdoor coffee table when he held up his pipe. "We weren't done marchin' yet," he said. I was confused. I'd assumed his ordeal was over when they reached Hagaru-ri.

Those survivors who had escaped to the east and south thought that they'd meet up in Hagaru-ri with others from the Eighth Army who'd done the same. Instead, when they reached the base, they learned that, of the 3300 soldiers of the Eighth Army sent to the east side of the Chosin, ninety percent had been wiped out.

"Ninety percent?" I exclaimed in dismay. Drummond only nodded. It was a long moment before he spoke again.

"We marched to the sea and they got us out on ships." We both sat in silence for another long moment.

What happens, I wondered, to a person who has witnessed inhumanity on this scale? Even after Drummond was evacuated on the SS Meredith from the port of Hungnam, his war, in many ways, would never be over. And now, even I would never look at him the same again. A wellspring had opened under him that I may have sensed before, but now had confirmed—the incomprehensible trauma that had influenced his life choices in every respect.

I later learned many more things about Drummond's war. No particular distinction was awarded to veterans of that conflict unless they were killed or wounded. It was years before even a lapel pin was minted to commemorate his campaign, and even more before there was a memorial in the nation's capital. Having survived this soul-shattering experience physically intact must have been an almost unbearable burden when so many were lost. Only those who survived with him would know. He was still looking to the treetops, and I wondered what more there could possibly be to add.

"I got home just in time for the 'leckshun," he said, almost smiling. Once again, I raced to scan my dates and history.

"The election? Was that when Eisenhower came in, Drum?"

"Yessah. Ike. No thanks to me."

My dessert was ready, and I needed to get up and tend to it, but I wanted to know what he meant by this. "You mean you didn't vote for him?"

"Couldn't."

"Couldn't? What do you mean, couldn't?"

"Weren't allowed to." I looked down at the Dutch oven, then back up at him. For the first time ever, my friend had just given me confirmation of something I'd long suspected. He was at least part Native.

When I lifted the Dutch oven by its bale, Drummond's gaze came back down to earth. I didn't know what to say. After having served his country in one of the most savage campaigns in one of its most brutal wars and survived it, he was denied the right to vote as a citizen of the country he fought for when he came home. I set the oven down on the stump and removed the lid. Drummond leaned forward to get a good look.

"Yessah!" he smiled. Then he inhaled deeply. "Wish I could grow pineapples, Chum." We both had a good laugh, and needed it. I picked up the oven and temporarily set it on the ground while I unrolled a piece of foil to spread over our coffee-table stump.

"I gutta see this," Drummond chuckled. I took out my red bandana from my back pocket. Using it as a potholder, I grasped one of the three feet on the bottom of the Dutch oven and hooked the bale with my stick. My practiced flip, with some extra flare, would either dazzle my audience of one, or we'd be picking pineapples and cake off the ground.

"Voila!" I croaked, when it landed intact, fruit side up. Drummond slapped his knee. The brown sugar had glazed the pineapples perfectly, and the cherries had darkened to a rich burgundy color.

"Yessah!" At that, he got up to retrieve the well-steeped tea, and I followed him in for some plates and forks. Outside again, I unsheathed my skinning knife and cut him a hefty slice.

"I thought about bringing some whipped cream, but I didn't think I'd be able to keep it cold for the trip."

"Whip some up yourself?"

"No, Drum. It comes in an aerosol can these days. You shake it and spray it on."

"Nossah!"

"Yep." I had to remind myself that whipped cream in an aerosol can wasn't around the last time Drummond Humchuck went into a grocery store. The last he knew, it still had to be whipped by hand from heavy cream in a bowl. Now he lit into his dessert robustly, savoring every morsel, as his gaze went skyward again.

"Second one a these I ever et," he smiled around a mouthful, clearly enjoying himself. "First warm one, though."

The rogue wave of memory had rolled out of my friend, and now the seas were calm again. We sipped our tea in silence, both letting the story settle, though I knew it would be churning in me for a long time to come. Later, when I researched it, I learned that Drummond was right—Native veterans returning from World War II and from the Korean conflict were still denied suffrage in the last two holdout states, Maine and Utah. I can't pretend to know what that felt like for him after what he'd been through on behalf of his country. Of the few things I've learned about my friend's life before Township Unknown, what he had shared this time had shaken me the most. I knew Drummond well enough not to ask questions right away, though my questions were bubbling up as I sat with him having tea. Those questions would all have been personal, and that's not how our relationship works. Things like that come out on their own, either when the spirit spontaneously moves, or when the right dessert shows up. Moreover, I knew so much more now than I'd ever known. I now knew that Drummond had experienced the painful ways in which prejudice came to bear on Native people. Had this been instrumental in his decision to live the way he does? It's not a question our relationship permits—not yet, anyway.

"So, the New York Public Library, Drum. You saw it?"

"Yessah! We come from San Francisco by rail. Had a stopover in New Yawk. 'Preciate the wood, chum." He meant the popsicle sticks and toothpicks with which he was recreating, from memory, that iconic landmark. It would most likely be finished the next time I came.

As I threaded my arms through the pack basket straps to leave, Drummond tried to convince me to take some of the pineapple upside-down cake with me. I wouldn't hear of it. I knew that the memories it had stirred would be around for at least as long as the cake lasted, and probably longer. I also knew that no Memorial Day would ever be the same for me again.

My hikes homeward were always reflective after my visits to Township Unknown. This time, the miles would evaporate under my feet. Some distance down the trail, after our long handshake and my promise to return soon, I heard something that stopped me in my tracks. There was wind high up in the hemlocks, but below that were the strains of a song, ricocheting through the forest. I sat. It took me a long moment to place it, but then I realized that what I was hearing was none other than "Vaya con Dios," made popular by Les Paul and Mary Ford in the early 1950s. It would have been on the radio when Drummond made his cross-country passage after his return from Korea. His mastery of the tune included not just the melody but also the plaintive, interwoven guitar figures that Les Paul played behind it. I wondered if my friend knew that I could hear him, that I was listening, along with every other living thing in that forest. I wondered if this song had been lying dormant along with everything else that had been awakened on this day. I knew one thing for sure: I'd never underestimate the power of a pineapple upside-down cake.

13
Carter Dodge

Carter Dodge became a resident of Grand Lake Stream by means of a time-honored process. In his former life, he was the head and horns of a high-powered ad agency on Madison Avenue in Manhattan, New York. One of the perks of that position was that, on occasion, a client would ask him along on some exotic getaway. For Carter, though, vacations were problematic. They caused him to feel off his game. So when he did accept an invitation that took him away from his work, he was keen to make sure that some business advantage was likely.

Once, he was on the verge of closing a deal with a big client—a deal he envisioned as the spores of spring cross-pollinating into many other successes. Everett Manning was the kind of mogul who could make careers with a few phone calls. At the last minute, when negotiations between Carter and Everett had matured well past the hopeful phase, Everett sprung something on Carter that completely disarmed him. He invited Carter on a wilderness expedition in a place he'd never heard of—Grand Lake Stream, Maine. They would "fish for landlocked salmon and smallmouth bass, do some white-water canoeing, and take in the wilds of Maine," according to Everett's email. They would stay in a rustic camp with gas lights and no indoor plumbing for five days!

At first, Carter wondered what kind of strategy this might be, for he viewed this move as he viewed everything—in a clinical light, as leverage and potential economic gain. He had long ago developed categories for his clients, convenient slots into which he deposited them, based on his long career of handling all the different psychological types. At length, he concluded that Everett Manning was the "touchy-feely" type—his least favorite. This type, before entering into a business association with someone, needed to satisfy emotional needs. They needed to have a "personal relationship" in order to give a "deeper meaning" to the business relationship. Personally, Carter had nothing but contempt for this group, but he had perfected the ability to pose as the same type. That, after all, was a characteristic of the consummate businessman—a chameleon-like capacity to change forms to suit the moment. He knew how to do all the glad-handing, spend "quality time," enter into "meaningful" discussions that had nothing to do with business, and in the end, triumph, just as he did with the opposite type—the realists like him, who took a jaundiced view of such nonsense and stuck to business.

Carter Dodge capitulated, but only to serve the greater cause of his eventual conquest. He took directions from Everett by email to make preparations for the trip. He made a list, and then instructed his secretary to order from L.L. Bean all the things he would need to rough it in the boondocks for five days. It was an investment he regretted having to make. There was virtually no possibility he would ever use this gear again. He was comfortable enough with his manhood and needed no Ernest Hemingway-type tests like this one to see how he measured up. Only a business victory would justify such frivolous spending. An advertising contract with Everett Manning, the New York commercial real estate giant, would justify everything.

In early June, the two men flew to Bangor International Airport, then shuttled to a nearby lake where a floatplane was waiting. Despite his misgivings about the trip, Carter felt himself to be in good form. Sincere-sounding laughter, banter about how important it was to periodically let down and have an "authentic experience," even some theatrical enthusiasm for what lay ahead—all these things were coming out of him as naturally as if they were heartfelt, and with his razor-sharp sixth sense, he was already picking up the scent of success.

That is, until the floatplane took off. Everett had insisted that Carter sit in the front seat for optimum visibility. They achieved an altitude of one thousand feet in only a few minutes. The experienced pilot, Tim, tipped his wing to starboard for Carter's sake, and Carter looked down. He saw the great expanses of spruce, pine, and fir forests, only interrupted by innumerable bodies of sparkling deep-blue water, in every conceivable shape and size. All at once, his stomach turned over, his eyes rolled back, and the blood drained out of his face. Tim instinctively righted the plane, reached into his door compartment, pulled out a sick bag, and handed it to him. Carter was violently ill, and even more violently embarrassed. He coughed and heaved into the bag until it was full, and the pilot handed him another. When there was nothing left to heave, he just groaned and attempted to clear his throat to form an apology. For the first time in Carter's professional life, he'd lost all composure.

"Not a problem," the pilot chimed in. "Happens to the best of 'em."

Then, adding to his mortification, Carter felt Everett's warm hand on his shoulder. "You OK now, Carter?"

He was still unable to speak. In fact, he didn't speak for the remainder of the thirty-minute flight, humiliated by the pungent stench in the cockpit that he'd caused. There were no more wing tips from Tim, and no more looking down for Carter Dodge.

Awful thoughts tore through Carter during those thirty minutes. The experience had blindsided him. When he'd looked down, it wasn't just the vertigo that overtook him. It was a visceral realization that he was completely out of his element. The world Carter had just left that morning, with its hum and buzz and smoke and smog, its screeching sirens and endless procession of hustling humanity, was familiar and comfortable. That was his element. The only life he knew was an over-scheduled one with no unaccountable time, and now he found himself in uncharted territory. What had he been thinking when he'd walked willingly into this trap?

Tim deftly stood on the pontoons and paddled the floatplane up alongside the town dock. Then he ducked under the wing and opened the passenger door. Carter was still pale. His first steps were tentative and shaky. Everett quickly jumped out beside him and put his arm around Carter's waist.

"You'll feel better in no time. Maybe a short nap in camp." Carter only nodded and let himself be led to a pickup truck owned by a friend of Everett's. They put their bags in back and followed a short dirt road that ran parallel to the lake, ending at their destination.

It was seven thirty in the evening. Carter still appeared shaken. He was unable to eat or drink anything. He stared out at the water, cocked his head strangely when he heard a loon call, and huddled in his chair. He appeared totally preoccupied and said almost nothing until he retired early. Everett wondered if he were witnessing a more serious illness than air sickness, perhaps some sort of a breakdown.

Carter attempted in vain to sleep. Of all things, the faces of his two former wives—both now remarried—rose in his mind's eye, and with this vision, a heaviness in his chest. Finally, sometime just before dawn, he fell asleep. In that short period of sleep, he dreamed that he was on the phone with an associate from his firm back in New York, but he himself was speaking from the cabin in Grand Lake Stream. In the dream, the associate was babbling indecipherably. As Carter held the receiver slightly away from his ear, he looked out from the camp porch at the sky over the water. A great charcoal-colored cloud that had completely covered the sky began to recede. Coming up from the horizon to replace this menacing mass was an ever-expanding band of blue. It grew and grew until he watched the last thin strip of dark gray disappear behind him. That was the end of the dream, and then he woke up.

The door to Carter's room was ajar when Everett came to check on him. He nudged it until he could glimpse the bed. Empty! "Good God," he said out loud, and all sorts of dire possibilities trammeled his brain. He raced around the camp looking out every window, and finally went out onto the screened porch. From there he saw Carter, standing on the dock with his hands in his pockets.

"Good morning, Mr. Dodge," he said.

Carter turned. "Good morning," he replied, and his voice sounded half an octave lower than it had the night before. "How big is this lake?" he asked as he looked back out on the water.

"Twelve miles long," Everett laughed. "And several miles wide, depending on where you're measuring."

"What—" Carter began, then paused—"do people do here?"

"Just what you're doing right now," Everett chuckled.

"Right," said Carter.

Carter's host was happy to see him devour a hearty breakfast of blueberry pancakes and venison sausage before going to meet their guide for the day at the Pine Tree Store. The minute Carter saw the man waiting for them, he remembered some of the L.L. Bean videos he'd watched online in his office.

"Haven't I seen you in a video?" he said to Sonny Sprague.

"Oh, I s'pose it's possible," Sonny said with a friendly smile. "You won't hold it against me, though, will ya?"

The two sports and their guide set out in Sonny's Grand Laker canoe for a place called the Gut, in Farm Cove. It took twenty-five minutes to get there, the volume of the Johnson outboard motor precluding much conversation. As always, Sonny used the time to study his sports, reaching his own conclusions long before they arrived in the Gut. One was clearly a first-timer, and one was not.

The day passed quickly. Fish were caught, a four-course shore lunch was cooked over an open fire, and before the day was through, Carter got to feel a salmon tugging on the other end of a fly rod. With coaching from both Everett and Sonny, he was able to bring the feisty fish alongside the canoe, where the sun reflected its shimmering blue and silver hues. At the last instant, the salmon lurched, ejected the fly from its mouth, and bolted away in a flash. All the way back to the camp, Carter appeared hypnotized. When they parted company at the Pine Tree Store, Sonny gave Carter a firm handshake and said, "You come back sometime, and we'll go back and get that salmon."

Everett had planned a full itinerary for their stay. The next day they canoed the St. Croix River along the Canadian border. It was a "bluebird day," no cloud cover at all. The day after that, they kayaked Grand Lake Stream. Everett Manning was delighting in the fact that everything they were doing was a first for Carter Dodge, the high-strung New York executive, and delighting, too, in how well he took to each adventure. He saw Carter feeling muscles he never knew he had. He saw him sleeping the sleep of the dead, and then waking up hungry for big breakfasts. When there was one day remaining, Carter asked his host if it would be all right if he just wiled away the day on his own. The day was free because Everett had planned it that way, hoping that precisely this would happen.

Carter walked out a trail called the Tower Road on the east side of the village and saw a doe deer on the way back. He went to the salmon hatchery and got a tour of the breeding pools. He dropped by the Pine Tree Store and bought a hat and a T-shirt, both with the Grand Lake Stream logo. For a long time, he sat on a rock at the lake shore, dangling his bare feet in the water. It wasn't so much that he was forcing a transformation on himself. It was more as if it was happening of its own accord, and he was powerless to resist it, even if he wanted to, which he didn't.

That evening, sitting on the porch of the rented camp, the two men watched the sunset, listened to loons, heard the *JUG-A-RUM!* of bullfrogs, and competed in conversation with a cacophony of crickets. Not a business word passed between them. Before retiring, Everett asked him if he thought he would be all right on the return floatplane ride. "I'd be happy to arrange for a car," he offered. Carter said not to worry; he'd be fine.

An hour later, when Carter was at the edge of sleep, he heard a voice call his name. He opened his eyes and waited, not sure if it had been in a dream. "Carter!" said the voice again, and it was coming from somewhere inside the camp. "Come see this!" He wrapped the top blanket around his shoulders and followed the sound to the porch. His host reached out one hand to pull Carter closer, and with the other hand pointed to the sky. "Northern Lights," he whispered, as though it were a transgression to speak too loudly in their presence. Carter wiped his eyes several times, until he realized he couldn't wipe away what he was seeing. When he finally focused on the dancing spokes of colored light beams, a shudder passed through his whole body. As if following a command, he walked down the porch steps to the lake shore, then out onto the dock. There he remained, fixated on the ever-changing light patterns which eventually encompassed more than half the night sky. As one ecstatic convulsion of light after another spoked upward, he felt the image boring into him deeply, and knew that it would be with him permanently.

From the moment he walked into the office the first morning back, everything looked different. And was it his imagination, or were people in the office looking at him oddly? Then he became fixated on the fact that, no matter where people were going or what they were doing, they were rushing, and the expressions on their faces seemed to indicate that whatever it was that was causing them to rush was of extreme importance. To be sure, these things had been true all along, but suddenly Carter was seeing all of it as if for the first time. Then, when he saw people looking at him strangely, the thought occurred to him that he might look different to them. A sensation of panic crept over him.

The worst part was actually getting down to work. When advertising copy came across his desk for his approval, he crossed out more than he left in because he saw almost all of it as ridiculous. To compound things, this former overachiever, famous for a numbing, robotic self-discipline, began to succumb to uncontrollable daydreaming! Every moment of his trip with Everett Manning played and replayed in his mind on a continuous loop. He stared out from his twenty-sixth-floor suite on Madison Avenue, and instead of seeing the blurred, seething heat rising from the teaming streets, instead of seeing the endless checkerboard of blocks and buildings competing for skyline, instead of seeing the carbon-tinged sprawl that stretched beyond his vision—he saw the blue and green of Grand Lake Stream. He saw that flashing salmon beside the boat before it plummeted to freedom. He saw the softened smile of Sonny Sprague, heard the waves lapping at rocks outside his cabin, and he conjured up the cricket symphonies of evening. Most of all, he saw the northern lights that had so impressed him on the final night of his stay. Though his body had returned to his former life, that life felt senseless and meaningless to him now.

Change was on a fast track. News came to Carter that an old friend and colleague from another ad agency in New York had gone into work the previous day, dropped down on the floor, and died. A team of EMTs worked on him, but it was too late. A massive heart attack had taken his friend at forty-nine, the same age as Carter.

Carter didn't sleep for a week. He went to work each day, bedraggled and frayed at the edges, unable to concentrate. The death of his friend and contemporary was a grim envoy of mortality, bearing an unwanted message. Now big questions confronted Carter, demanding answers. They began with "If the same thing happened to me," but he was afraid to think this through. He knew where it led. A month earlier, he might have said, "But what else is there?" Now he knew.

One more week, and his decision was made. Everyone would call him crazy. He already knew that. But the tide that carried him was simply too strong to fight. Life was short, and with whatever time that remained, he would listen more to his heart and less to his head. He resolved to keep everything to himself until the very last minute. Luckily, he rented instead of owned a New York high-rise apartment, and his lease was almost up for renewal anyway. He called Everett Manning and got the name of a Grand Lake Stream realtor. Carter's company had in fact won a contract with Manning's company, so when Everett took Carter's call, he understood completely what was happening. Finally, Carter contacted a business broker to put his agency on the market.

Once he'd tied up these loose ends, things were propelled as though by a fateful tailwind. Carter gave in to the flow. With the help of faxes, printouts, and pictures, he picked out a small home within the village of Grand Lake Stream. It was fully outfitted for year-round living. It never once occurred to him, the consummate businessman, to quibble about the sale price.

One month from the day he made his decision, everything was set. His business broker had come through with a handsome offer on Carter's successful, reputable agency, and once again, he didn't quibble. On a Monday morning, he made the announcement at work that he would be leaving the firm and moving to rural Maine. A shock wave went through the twenty-sixth floor, which was only partially alleviated by the news that the new owner of the agency would keep everyone on staff. At the water cooler, people agreed that Mr. Dodge had indeed been looking and acting strange of late. Perhaps this was his late mid-life crisis, or worse—maybe he'd received some grim diagnosis.

A late-model Jeep Cherokee with New York plates and a U-Haul trailer went over Musquash Bridge, about six miles outside of Grand Lake Stream, on a sunny June afternoon.

Perched like sentinels at the gates of town, two enormous ravens sat in the fork of a birch tree beside the bridge, craning their necks as if to scrutinize the newcomer passing below.

In town, Carter recognized the house from the faxed pictures. It still had a For Sale sign in front, but he knew it was the right one, and he let out an uncharacteristic yelp as he turned into the drive. The small log-sided house was clean, neat, and had a crisp, woodsy smell which agreed with Carter. On the kitchen counter he found a friendly note of greeting from the realtor. She also wrote that she'd pick up the For Sale sign in a day or two.

With the contents of the Jeep unloaded, Carter decided to make up a bed and not worry about the U-Haul until the next morning. Instead, he drove to the Pine Tree Store and bought a six-pack of beer, something he hadn't done in twenty years. Sitting on his new porch, he listened to the last birds of evening, wood thrushes, whose song only subsided when the swelling sounds of peep frogs came from all directions. Well past twilight and three beers in, he heard the first reports of bullfrogs from a nearby swamp.

After going to bed and falling into a deep sleep, the dream began. It was his life, depicted in an ad agency commercial, one that he had produced. He saw himself as one of millions of Manhattan marionettes, tied to the strings of financial security. He saw himself worshipping the stock market, watching it go up and down even as he went up and down, to and from his high-rise apartment, day after day, never noticing the losses, the loves, the life that might have happened while he was keeping his eye on the bouncing ball. He had chased that bouncing ball of fortune for thirty years, and the dream showed that his sacrifices were profound. Then the face of his friend, the one whose recent death had acted as a catalyst, appeared. He was smiling broadly, and that's when Carter realized they were in a floatplane together.

After unloading the U-Haul the next morning, he decided he'd try to look up Sonny Sprague, the only person he knew in his new town. Carter Dodge became a resident of Grand Lake

Stream, Maine, joining a legion of others throughout its history who'd arrived before him in the same way and for the same reasons.

Gradually, that other world fell away. It wasn't just that it left his thoughts, which were so busy with new possibilities and dreams. It was leaving his body too. Slowly but surely, there was a relaxing of tensions that he used to think of as normal. He thought it would sound crazy to any of his old associates, but he actually believed his hearing was improving. Instead of a din of urban noise, he was discerning different sounds now, differentiating between the sound of the stream, ever-present in town, and that of the wind, waxing and waning. He became interested in birds and critters of all kinds. Better to say he noticed them now.

Carter surrendered to the transformation. He didn't know where it led; he was in brand-new territory now. All he knew was that he was now listening to something that came from himself rather than somewhere else. He'd follow it into an unknown future because, for the first time in his life, what he was listening to felt true.

About the Author

RANDY SPENCER guides fishermen on the Canadian border waters of Downeast Maine. He has written two award-winning books. His first, *Where Cool Waters Flow: Four Seasons with a Master Maine Guide* won the New England Outdoors 2010 Book of the Year award. His second, *Wide and Deep: Tales and Recollections of a Master Maine Fishing Guide* won the same award for 2015, as well as Best contemporary nonfiction of 2015 from the New England Society in the City of New York. In addition, *Wide and Deep* won National First Prize in Nonfiction from the Outdoor Writers Association of America.

Randy has been named one of the Ten Most Intriguing People in Maine by *Portland Magazine*. *Yankee Magazine* included him as one of the 25 people you need to meet most. He has been the subject of features on CBS Sunday Morning, Boston's WCVB-TV's *Chronicle*, *The Wall Street Journal*, and ESPN2.

Randy, his wife Shelley, and their two English Springer Spaniels, divide their time between Grand Lake Stream and Holden, Maine.

CPSIA information can be obtained
at www.ICGtesting.com
Printed in the USA
BVHW091632261021
619923BV00017B/507